CAMBRIDGE FIRST CERTIFICATE
Reading

NEW EDITION

Paul Roberts

CAMBRIDGE
UNIVERSITY PRESS

PUBLISHED BY THE PRESS SYNDICATE OF THE UNIVERSITY OF CAMBRIDGE
The Pitt Building, Trumpington Street, Cambridge, United Kingdom

CAMBRIDGE UNIVERSITY PRESS
The Edinburgh Building, Cambridge CB2 2RU, UK
40 West 20th Street, New York, NY 10011–4211, USA
477 Williamstown Road, Port Melbourne, VIC 3207, Australia
Ruiz de Alarcón 13, 28014 Madrid, Spain
Dock House, The Waterfront, Cape Town 8001, South Africa

http://www.cambridge.org

First published 1994
Second edition 1999
Reprinted 2001, 2002 (Twice)

Printed in the United Kingdom at the University Press, Cambridge

ISBN 0 521 64656 1 Student's Book
ISBN 0 521 64655 3 Teacher's Book

Contents

Map of the book

Introduction

Who is this book for?

Cambridge First Certificate Reading is for learners who need additional practice in reading skills in preparation for Paper 1 of the Cambridge First Certificate in English (FCE) examination. As the book aims to improve learners' reading skills in general, as well as specifically for the exam, it can also be used appropriately by non-exam learners at upper intermediate level who want to develop their reading ability.

How is it organised?

The *Student's Book* is organised into learning units and practice tests. The learning units present different techniques for acquiring useful reading skills and the practice tests provide an opportunity to test those skills in the context of Paper 1 of the FCE exam.

There are fifteen learning units and five practice tests. In addition, a Foundation unit at the beginning presents the subskills necessary for developing and improving reading skills at this level and a Review unit at the end summarises and consolidates all the reading techniques presented in the book. Five broad themes run through all the learning units and practice tests, loosely linking the material together.

Each learning unit focuses on a different set of reading skills and on a specific part of the Paper 1 exam. Summary boxes at the beginning of each unit give clear information about the unit's skills and exam coverage and provide cross-references to relevant practice test material. Exam tip boxes in every unit provide a useful summary of key techniques.

The practice test material closely resembles Paper 1 of the FCE exam and includes examples of all variations of the exam format.

The *Teacher's Book* contains a timing guide for each unit, detailed teaching notes and a key to the unit exercises and practice tests.

How should the material be used?

The learning units are intended to be used in sequence because reading techniques and exam skills are built up gradually and an element of recycling and revision is incorporated into the book. It is, however, possible to choose individual units for particular skills practice or particular exam part practice, as each unit is self-contained and can stand alone. Each learning unit provides between 40 and 60 minutes' work.

The practice tests can be used flexibly, in conjunction with or independently of the learning units. Test parts can be used in any order, individually or as a complete test:

- to check progress or to provide authentic timed exam practice.
- after every four learning units or at other intervals throughout the course.
- for homework or in class.
- with students working individually or in pairs/groups.

Foundation unit

What sort of things do you read?

What sort of things do you read in your own language? What do you read in English?

Look at the chart below. The things people read are called 'text types'.

Text type	Page number
newspaper article	
non-fiction book	
magazine article	
story	
brochure	
biography	

Work with another student. Go through the book quickly and glance at the texts on pages 11, 15, 19, 23, 27, 32, 35, 40, 43, 48, 51, 55, 60, 62 and 67.

Can you say which text type each piece of reading is just by looking at it?

Write the page numbers on the chart, next to each text type. Then discuss these questions with two or three other students.

1 Which of the text types do you like reading?
2 Which of them do you have to read (even if you don't like reading them)?
3 Which do you never read? Why?
4 Are there any other sorts of text you sometimes read?

FIRST CERTIFICATE EXAM

There are four parts in Paper 1 of the exam. In each part, you have to read one or more texts. The texts in Paper 1 could be any of the types in the list above. Sometimes you might have to read a guide book, a manual or an information leaflet, sometimes an advertisement, a letter or a report. In your general English reading, try to read different text types – even those you don't enjoy!

Different kinds of reading

Work with another student. Discuss what is different about the way you read a timetable and the way you read a novel.

Which of the text types below do you normally read in the same way as you read a novel? Which the same way as a timetable? Fill in the chart.

magazine article   encyclopaedia entry   research article   guide book
manual   newspaper article   letter from a friend   brochure   biography

Things we read like a novel	*Things we read like a timetable*

FIRST CERTIFICATE EXAM

Different parts of the exam involve different tasks and different kinds of reading. Part 1 is a multiple matching task – you have to match headings or summary sentences to the paragraphs in the text. In Part 2 you have to answer multiple choice comprehension questions. In Part 3 you have to complete gapped text with missing sentences or paragraphs. Part 4 is another multiple matching task – you have to match particular information you are given before you read to the relevant section(s) of text. Parts 1, 2 and 3 all test how well you can read and understand the writer's message. Part 4 tests your ability to read and extract specific information.

How can you become a better reader?

1 You can become a better reader by learning to deal with difficult words.

Read the text below. It contains some invented words. Try to guess their meaning.

> The journey into town took less than ten minutes; it was a quarter past three when Stella arrived in Houghton Street. She picked up her <u>blistable</u> radio, <u>squarked</u> from the taxi and ran to the door in a <u>flort</u>. If she had given herself time to think, paused to thank the driver or to <u>plinge</u> her hair, she might have run off in the opposite direction and wasted her moment for ever.

Discuss these questions with another student.

1 Do you agree about the probable meaning of the invented words?
2 Did any parts of the unknown words help you to guess their meaning?

FIRST CERTIFICATE EXAM

All the reading texts in the exam may contain some words which you do not understand. Some of the exercises in this book will help you guess the meaning of difficult words and show you how to understand the passage without having to understand all the words.

---

2 You can become a better reader by ignoring irrelevant information.

Look at the advertisement and answer the question.

How much does it cost to change oil at the service centre?

WHILE – U – WAIT
SERVICE CENTRE

Motor repairs at competitive prices

| Clutch – Silencer – Brake pads – Welding |
| Tyre alignment – Puncture repair – Timing belts |

Free oil change with most services

<u>FREEPHONE 0500 807993</u>

How many new words were there in the advertisement?

Could you answer the question? How quickly?

FIRST CERTIFICATE EXAM

In Part 4 of the exam you have to read quickly for specific information. In order to do this, you should not let difficult words get in the way. This book will help you with ways of ignoring irrelevant information.

3 You can become a better reader by getting an overall picture before you start reading intensively.

Read the text below. Then discuss these questions with another student.

1 Which is the *correct floor*?
2 What is the *whole operation*?
3 How far is *that far*?

> If the balloons popped, the sound would not be able to carry because everything would be too far away from the correct floor. Since the whole operation depends on electricity, a break in the middle of the wire would also cause problems. The man could shout, but the human voice is probably not loud enough to carry that far.

Have you given up? It's impossible to answer the questions! Now look at the picture on the next page, read the text again and try to answer the same questions.

FIRST CERTIFICATE EXAM

In order to understand the texts in Parts 1–3 of the exam, you must first get a general idea of what they are about. Some texts have pictures with them and many have titles which will help you. There is always some information about text type and subject in the instructions at the beginning. This book will help you with other ways of getting a general idea about texts before reading them intensively.

In Part 4 of the exam, there is always a detailed introduction to the type of text you have to read. You do not have to read intensively. It is not, therefore, so necessary to use a particular technique to get a general idea.

4 You can become a better reader by responding to the text.

Try this activity.

a) Read the question and instruction after the letter e).
b) It is the one in Central America, beginning with 'M'. Now read the instruction after the letter d).
c) Tokyo, Jakarta, London, Mexico City, New York. Look at letter b) for the right answer.
d) How did you show you understood what you read in letters a), e), c) and b)? Look at the letter f).
e) Which is the largest city in the world? For some possibilities, look at the letter c).
f) You showed you understood by responding to the instructions – you did something as a result of reading.

FIRST CERTIFICATE EXAM

Most of our reading is not instructions – we don't usually have to do anything. But in order to understand properly, we must respond. In the exam, getting the right answer very often depends on having the right response to the text. In Part 4 of the exam, you will be told how to respond, but in the other parts it will be up to you.

Discuss the responses you might have to different text types with another student. Look at the chart below. How many responses might you have to each text type?

Text type	Response
newspaper article	take notes for future use
non-fiction book	tell someone about it
magazine article	look at a map or picture
story	think carefully
biography	try to learn something
research article	smile, be sad or excited
guide book	look at the last page

5 You can become a better reader by analysing the text very carefully.

Read the short text below. Then discuss the questions with another student.

> The English don't often complain in restaurants. They don't like to attract attention. So they might, for example, write a letter a day or two after the event.

1 Which linking word could you put before *They don't*?
a) While   b) Therefore   c) However   d) Because

2 What does *So* mean?
a) Therefore   b) In order that   c) As

3 What is *the event*?

FIRST CERTIFICATE EXAM

To complete some items in Parts 1–3 of the exam you will have to analyse a short section of the text very closely. This will require you to understand the meaning of the 'linking' words and to see how parts of the sentence relate to each other. You cannot do this without looking at the sentence in the context of the whole text.

6 You can become a better reader by keeping your purpose in mind.

Read the short text below.

> One of the many special work schemes for young men and women involves spending five months as a Park Ranger in the Coaguaza National Park in Paraguay. The park is located 335 kilometres from Asunción, Paraguay's capital. The park is remote: the last 150 kilometres are along a tortuous, unpaved road and, once inside, the only communication with the outside world is through infrequent contact with the Park Director's office in Asunción. The work provides a glimpse into the life and rhythms of the rain forest: it involves cataloguing varieties of flora and fauna and creating exhibits for the park's museum. The job provides an opportunity to gain contact with the Guarani culture and to become fluent in Spanish.

Now answer this question.

How long does the Park Ranger work last?

If you had seen this question before you looked at the text, how would your reading have been affected?

FIRST CERTIFICATE EXAM

In Part 4 of the exam you will be given a reading purpose before you look at the text. In this book you will find ways to help you to keep your purpose in mind as you read.

Testing your progress – the First Certificate in English exam

Paper 1 in the exam

The four parts of Paper 1 always appear in the same order in the exam and each part always features the same task:

- Part 1 is a multiple matching task – you have to match headings or summary sentences to paragraphs in the text. There are usually six or seven items in Part 1.
- In Part 2 you have to answer multiple choice comprehension questions. There are usually seven or eight questions in this part of the exam, each with four answers to choose from.
- In Part 3 you have to complete a gapped text by inserting the missing sentences or paragraphs at the correct point in the text. There are usually six or seven items in this part of the exam.
- Part 4 is another multiple matching task. This time you are given particular information to look for and must choose the section(s) of text where it can be found. There are usually thirteen to fifteen items in this part of the exam.

You have 75 minutes to do Paper 1 in the exam.

Practice tests

At the end of the book (pages 78–117), there are five practice tests. They are very similar to Paper 1 in the FCE exam.

Look at the five tests now and answer these questions.

1 How many questions are there in total in Paper 1?
2 Which parts of the exam have an example and what number question is it?
3 Which parts of the exam have an extra answer which you do not need to use?
4 In which part of the exam can you use an answer more than once?
5 Which part of the exam sometimes has more than one answer for the same question?

FIRST CERTIFICATE EXAM

Remember that this book can't do your reading for you! It is up to you to read – and not just this book! Read as many books, newspapers, magazines, notices, letters – in fact anything at all – as you possibly can. Use the techniques that this book introduces to help you read more efficiently. If you are an efficient reader you will be successful in the exam. Good luck!

Unit 1 The fun they had

Reading skills: Getting an overall picture from words which occur again and again

Dealing with difficult words by concentrating on the words you do understand

Responding to the text by trying to 'hear' dialogue

Exam focus: Part 2 Multiple choice comprehension questions

Theme: Education – see page 104 for a Part 2 practice test on the same theme

Getting an overall picture

1 Look at the text on the opposite page. You have one minute to note down any words which appear again and again.

Now check with another student. Did you note the same words?

2 The text is about schools in the year 2157. Discuss this question with your partner.

In what ways do you think schools will be different in the year 2157?

Use the chart to note down your ideas.

	Schools now	*Schools in 2157*
subjects studied		
teaching methods		
organisation		
other		

Discuss this question with another student.

Do you think schools in 2157 will be better or worse than they are now or will they be about the same?

EXAM TIP 1

Remember that it is difficult to read a text if you do not first have an overall picture. You may understand little and get into a panic! One way to get an overall picture is to look quickly at the text for words which occur again and again.

The fun they had

by I. Asimov

Margie even wrote about it that night in her diary. On the page headed May 17, 2157, she wrote, 'Today Tommy found a real book!'

It was a very old book. Margie's grandfather once said that there was a time when all stories were printed on paper.

5 They turned the pages, which were yellow and delicate, and it was awfully funny to read words that stood still instead of moving about the way they were supposed to – on a screen, you know.

She said, 'Where did you find it?'

'In my house.' He pointed without looking, because he was busy reading. 'In the cellar.'

'What's it about?'

10 'School.'

Margie was scornful. 'School? What's there to write about school? I hate school … Why would anyone write about school?'

Tommy looked at her with very superior eyes. 'Because it's not our kind of school, stupid. This is the old kind of school that they had hundreds and hundreds of years ago.' He added grandly,

15 pronouncing the word carefully, '*Centuries* ago.'

Margie was hurt. 'Well, I don't know what kind of school they had all that time ago.' She read the book over his shoulder for a while, then said, 'Anyway, they had a teacher.'

'Sure they had a teacher, but it wasn't a *regular* teacher. It was a man.'

'A man? How could a man be a teacher?'

20 'Well, he just told the boys and girls things and gave them homework and asked them questions.'

'A man isn't clever enough.'

'Sure he is. My father knows as much as my teacher.'

'He can't. A man can't know as much as a teacher.'

'He knows almost as much.'

25 Margie wasn't prepared to argue about that. She said, 'I wouldn't want a strange man in my house to teach me.'

Tommy screamed with laughter. 'You don't know much, Margie. The teachers didn't live in the house. They had a special building and all the kids went there.'

'And all the kids learned the same thing?'

30 'Sure, if they were the same age.'

'But my mother says a teacher has to be made to fit the mind of each boy and girl it teaches and that each kid has to be taught differently.'

'Just the same they didn't do it that way then. If you don't like it, you don't have to read the book.'

35 'I didn't say I didn't like it,' Margie said quickly. She wanted to read about those funny schools. They weren't even half-finished when Margie's mother called, 'Margie! School!'

Margie went into the schoolroom. It was right next to her bedroom, and the mechanical teacher was on and waiting for her.

The screen was lit up, and it said, 'Today's arithmetic lesson is on the addition of proper

40 fractions. Please put yesterday's homework in the proper drive.'

Margie did so with a sigh. She was thinking about the old schools they had when her grandfather's grandfather was a little boy. All the kids from the whole neighbourhood came, laughing and shouting in the schoolyard, sitting together in the same schoolroom, going home together at the end of the day. They learned the same things, so they could help one another on the

45 homework and talk about it.

And the teachers were people …

Dealing with difficult words

1 Read the first four lines of the text on the previous page. Discuss these questions with another student.

    1 Who are the people in the story?
    2 What do you think they have instead of real books?
    3 What do you think the real book was like?
    4 How did Margie feel about the discovery of the real book?

2 Read as far as line 6 of the text. As you read, underline everything you understand. Yes, everything you understand!

Compare your text with another student.

    1 Have you underlined the same parts of the text?
    2 Which words did you leave without underlining?
    3 Did these words stop you from understanding the story?

EXAM TIP 2

New words in a text can make you unnecessarily worried. Keep your confidence in the exam by concentrating on what you do understand. One way to do this is to underline the text as you read it. Go back and think about the meanings of new words, the ones you did not underline, only when you've finished reading and understanding.

Responding to the text

1 Read the text as far as line 17. As you read, pick out the dialogue between Margie and Tommy. (Use a highlighting pen if you have one at hand. You could even use different coloured pens to highlight Margie's and Tommy's lines.) Then circle any words which tell you how Margie and Tommy speak.

2 Work with two other students. One person will read the part of Margie, another will read the part of Tommy and the third will be the director. The director must tell the others how to read their parts. Use the words you have circled to help you.

EXAM TIP 3

Remember that you must respond to the text in order to read it efficiently. When you are reading fiction, you can do this by trying to 'hear' dialogue.

Exam practice: Part 2 Multiple choice comprehension questions

Finish reading the text. Then try to answer this question.

Why did Margie sigh? (line 41)

Look at these four possible answers to the question. Which one corresponds most closely to your answer?

A She wasn't keen on arithmetic.
B She wanted to finish reading the book.
C She would have preferred a different kind of school.
D She was upset that she had argued with Tommy.

EXAM TIP 4

In Part 2 of the exam, try to answer multiple choice questions in your own words first, before looking at the four given answers.

Extension

Discuss these questions with another student.

1 When do you prefer to study alone?
2 What are the benefits of studying with other people?
3 Do you sometimes use a computer to study English? What are the advantages and disadvantages of learning by computer?
4 Do you think that computers could replace human teachers?
5 How do you imagine schooling will take place in the near future? And in the distant future?

Unit 2 Choosing a college place

In this unit you are going to read an extract from a brochure for Bedford College.

Keeping your purpose in mind

1 The following people are all interested in going to Bedford College. Look at their specific needs. If you were about to go to college, which person's needs would seem most similar to your own?

1

I don't want to teach but I would like to work with children in the community.

2

It's been a long time since I was at school: I need to get the right certificates so that I can then get into a university.

3

I'm very interested in cooking and want something which will help me to get a job in that area.

4

I don't just want to learn theory – I'd really like the chance to see how things work in practice in a real working environment like an office or a factory.

5

What I want to do is run a big company one day: I'm looking for a course which might help me in that direction.

2 Use these key words and expressions to help you remember the students' needs. Match one to each student.

    Children   Catering   Management   Work experience   Entrance qualifications

3 Work with another student and have a reading race. Start reading the text below as quickly as you can. See who is the first to find a word or phrase connected to one of the needs you have summarised.

EXAM TIP 5

In Part 4 of the examination you will be given a list of specific information to look for. Try to summarise each piece of information with one or two words before you read. This will help you keep your reading purpose in mind while you read.

Access courses

Access courses provide an opportunity for adults over 21 to return to study and to prepare themselves for diploma or degree level study in a way which is thoroughly adult. Many successful access course students have gone on to study to become teachers, midwives, social workers, physiotherapists and radiologists, and many others have chosen degrees in a wide range of subjects,
5 leading to possibilities they never dreamed of when starting with us.

All Bedford College access courses are recognised nationally as giving successful students the qualifications they need in order to enter higher education.

The range of courses gets wider every year and a new venture this year is outreach access, which brings Bedford College's expertise and opportunities to other communities.

Advanced and professional

10 In the professional area, the college delivers programmes at different levels and in a variety of subjects, principally to support people seeking to make rapid progress in their careers. These include courses in general management, accountancy, personnel, marketing, purchasing and supply, quality management, administrative management and teacher education.

We have very strong links with de Montfort University and students on advanced and professional
15 courses have access to the university's facilities and activities.

The staff teaching our advanced and professional courses are well-qualified and committed, and have recent commercial experience. A feature of our programme is the high level of tutorial support which is available for all students.

Creative arts

Our expanding range of catering courses offers you the opportunity either to take a broad path
20 developing practical and supervisory skills, or to concentrate on a specific interest or skill, perhaps in one of the newly developed specialisms of vegetarian and international cuisine.

Careers in hairdressing and beauty are suitable for all age groups – you could work on a cruise liner, in a hotel, health centre, hospital or salon, or be your own boss. Diplomas in hairdressing and beauty provide an excellent preparation for work, whichever environment you choose.

25 Two new courses are starting this year. Media: Communication and Production will include print graphics, photography and audio-visual work with film, TV, animation and broadcasting. The National Diploma in Performing Arts will allow students to develop their talents through acting, directing, movement and stage craft.

Health and leisure

Caring for children in the home, in hospital and in residential settings, nurseries and schools
30 requires trained people. With our range of courses you have the best of all possible worlds: you gain practical skills and accreditation for them, as well as the theoretical knowledge you need to underpin your practice.

Students in health and social care focus on the community and its health and care support services. Many students when they leave go into professional training in such areas as nursing, occupational
35 therapy or social work.

Leisure and tourism qualifications can lead to careers in sport and leisure centres, health clubs, outdoor centres, theme parks, holiday organisations and various forms of community recreation.

Technology

Computing is a large and complex industry in itself, but, more importantly, the application of computers in the modern business world and in all walks of life is recognised as a major growth
40 area, and the demand for trained and flexible staff remains strong.

We have strong and established links with local industry. During your course you will have the opportunity to visit particular companies to enable you to relate your studies to current industrial practices.

Our teaching staff are qualified technologists, all with substantial industrial experience, supported
45 by expert technical staff in laboratories, workshops and computer areas. Our main concern is teaching and care of students; we'll want you to work hard, but we also believe that technology should be fun and we'll try to give you all the help and support you need to ensure that your time with us is both successful and enjoyable.

Ignoring irrelevant information

Read the whole text as quickly as you can. Underline or highlight words or phrases which correspond to the students' needs you summarised.

EXAM TIP 6

Use highlighting or underlining to mark the relevant sections of the text. This will help you to go back over it to check information without wasting time with irrelevant information.

Exam practice: Part 4 Multiple matching

Match each student's needs to the appropriate heading in the brochure. Write the relevant heading in each space.

1	
2	
3	
4	
5	

Extension

Work with another student or in a small group. Imagine you are choosing which college to go to. Put the criteria below in order of importance. Write 1 next to the most important and 6 next to the least important.

Fully qualified staff ☐

Staff with additional, non-educational experience ☐

Good facilities ☐

Tutorial help and support ☐

Recognised qualifications for successful students ☐

Recommended by former students ☐

Still with your partner(s), discuss these questions.

1 If you had the opportunity to study something new, which subject or area would you choose?
2 Are there any areas of study in the brochure extract that you read which you would not find in a college or university in your country?

Unit 3 Schools keep boys and girls apart

Reading skills:	Getting an overall picture from the title and illustration
	Responding to the text by relating it to personal experience
	Analysing the text: reference words
Exam focus:	Part 3 Gapped text
Theme:	Education – see page 98 for a Part 3 practice test on the same theme

Getting an overall picture

Look at the text on the opposite page. You have one minute to read the title and study the graph.

Discuss these questions with another student.

1 Does the text come from a story, a non-fiction book, a newspaper or a brochure?
2 What do you think is the answer to the question in the title of the text?

EXAM TIP 7

Remember always to try to get an overall picture before you start reading intensively. Use illustrations and titles to start you thinking about what the text is about. Combine this with the technique of looking for words which occur again and again, which you practised in Unit 1.

Responding to the text

Read the text carefully. When you see the sign ✳, stop reading and relate the ideas you have read about to your own experience by answering these questions.

✳1 Is/Was it like this at your school?
✳2 Do you think this is true in nursery schools in your country?

✳3 Is/Was this true of your teachers?
✳4 Do you agree?

When you have finished reading the whole text, discuss your reactions to the text with another student. Talk about your school(s) and your teachers.

EXAM TIP 8

Remember that you can understand texts better if you respond to them. It is often possible to relate the text to your own experience, especially with non-fiction. This is one of the best ways of responding.

Why do boys achieve more than girls in science and mathematics?

If there is no difference in general intelligence between boys and girls, what can explain girls' lack of success in science and mathematics?

It seems to be that their treatment at school is a direct cause. Mathematics and science are seen as mainly masculine subjects, and therefore, as girls become teenagers, they are
5 less likely to take them. Interestingly, both boys and girls tend to regard the 'masculine' subjects as more difficult. Yet it has been suggested that girls avoid mathematics courses, not because they are difficult, but for social reasons. Girls do not want to be in open competition with boys because they are afraid to appear less feminine and attractive. *1

However, if we examine the performance of boys and girls who have undertaken
10 mathematics courses, there are still more high-achieving boys than there are girls. This difference appears to be world-wide (see graph). Biological explanations have been offered for this, but there are other explanations too.

Perhaps the difference which comes out during the teenage years has its roots in much earlier experiences. From their first days in nursery school, males are encouraged to work
15 on their own and to complete tasks. *2   Evidence shows that exceptional mathematicians and scientists have not had teachers who supplied answers.

Apart from that, there can be little doubt that teachers of mathematics and science expect their male students to do better at these subjects than their female students. *3   They even appear to encourage the difference between the sexes. They spend more time with the
20 male students, giving them longer to answer questions and working harder to get correct responses from them. They are more likely to call on boys for answers and to allow them to take the lead in classroom discussion. They also praise boys more frequently. All of this tends to encourage boys to work harder in science and mathematics and to give them confidence that they are able to succeed. *4

25 Such male-oriented teaching is not likely to encourage girls to take many mathematics and science courses, nor is it likely to support girls who do. It seems certain, then, that where these subjects are concerned, school widens the difference between boys and girls.

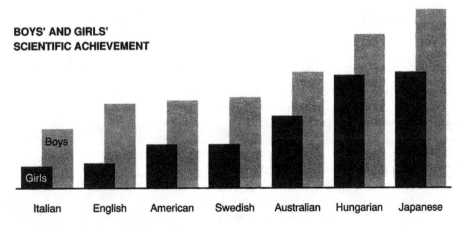

BOYS' AND GIRLS' SCIENTIFIC ACHIEVEMENT

Boys

Girls

Italian   English   American   Swedish   Australian   Hungarian   Japanese

▲ Boys have better science achievement scores; across the world there is a consistent sex difference.

Analysing the text

1 Look at the following sentence from lines 10–11 of the text.

> This difference appears to be world-wide.

It is impossible to understand this sentence without reading the sentence before it, because it refers to the previous sentence.

This difference refers to the fact that in mathematics there are more high-achieving boys than girls.

It can be useful to show what 'reference words' refer to like this:

> However, if we examine the performance of boys and girls who have undertaken mathematics courses, [there are still more high-achieving boys than girls]. (This difference) appears to be world-wide.

2 Find this phrase in line 26 of the text and discuss the questions with another student.

> nor is it likely to support girls who do

1 What is the difference between *nor* and *or*?
2 What does *it* refer to?
3 Can you replace *do* with a complete phrase? (Start with a main verb.)

Using the same method as before, you can show what *it* and *do* refer to:

> [Such male-oriented teaching] is not likely to encourage girls to [take many mathematics and science courses], nor is (it) likely to support girls who (do).

3 Circle the following reference words and phrases in the text.

their (line 3)
they (line 4)
this (line 12)
that (line 17)
these subjects (line 18)
them (line 20)
this (line 22)
Such male-oriented teaching (line 25)

Show what they refer to in the same way as above.

EXAM TIP 9

In Part 3 of the exam you will have to insert missing sentences or paragraphs into a gapped text. In order to do this effectively, you need to analyse the text and to pay close attention to any words which could refer to previous ideas.

Exam practice: Part 3 Gapped text

Look again at the numbered spaces in the text. They are the points, marked ✳, where you responded to the text on page 18.

Choose from the sentences below the one which fits each numbered space. Use your text analysis skills to help you.

A This is essential behaviour for learning how to solve problems later on.

B They do not do this consciously, but they still do it.

C This belief is the key to their actual success.

D Nor, it seems, do they want to draw attention to themselves.

Extension

Discuss these questions with another student.

1 What changes would you make in your country's education system to help more women become mathematicians and scientists?

2 Are there any jobs in your country which are generally done by women? How are men discouraged from taking these jobs?

3 Do you think that boys might achieve less success at school in languages and the humanities? If so, why do you think it might be?

Unit 4 Defending your territory on the beach

Getting an overall picture

1 Look at the title of the text on the opposite page. Discuss these questions with another student.

   1 What do you normally associate with the words *defend* and *territory*?
   2 How do people defend territory?
   3 How do you know where one person's (or one country's) territory ends and another's begins?
   4 How do people defend their territory on beaches?

2 Discuss your last beach holiday with another student. Talk about any problems you had with crowded beaches, and the sort of things you took with you to the beach.

EXAM TIP 10

Often the easiest and most obvious technique for getting an overall picture of a text is to read the title and think very carefully about what it means. The texts you will have to read in the exam nearly always have a title which helps you to get an overall picture.

Dealing with difficult words

In the text you are about to read you will find the expression *passers-by* (line 48). How can you work out what it means if you've never seen the expression before?

1 Divide the expression into different parts like this: *passers-by = pass + er + s + by*.
2 What does the *-er* ending mean? Think of *driver* and *player*.
3 You know the meaning of *pass* and *by*. So what do you think *passers-by* means? Yes, *passers-by* are people who *pass by*.

The following words or expressions also appear in the text. If you have difficulty understanding them, try dividing them into parts to help you guess their meanings.

belongings (line 2)   air-beds (line 3)   equidistant (line 23)
by-passed (lines 49–50)   thereafter (line 55)

EXAM TIP 11

Remember to concentrate on what you do understand. You may be able to guess the meaning of new words by breaking them down into parts.

Wall + Paper = Wallpaper

DEFENDING YOUR TERRITORY ON THE BEACH

1

The first thing to note is the range of personal belongings that individuals take with them to the beach – the air-beds, beach umbrellas, radios and towels. Whole families arrive totally
5 weighed down with their possessions. They go to a lot of trouble to get them to the beach, lugging huge, heavy umbrellas hundreds of yards or more from their hotel or from their car.

2

10 Sometimes you can watch a family group for a whole day and discover that not one member of the group has ever sat in the shade below the umbrella which was so heavy and difficult to carry in the first place. Underwater swimming
15 gear has been carried all the way from the hotel and yet no-one ever went underwater

swimming. All this equipment has been merely brought to the beach to mark out the new territorial boundaries of this family group. It forms a fence through which strangers cannot pass 20 without first having been invited.

3

And then there is the question of spacing. The goal seems to be to find a spot equidistant from those already occupying the beach. You can almost see some people doing the various cal- 25 culations in their head to work out the right spot, an equal distance from those already there. Having worked out the spot, they then plant the umbrella, as if they were planting a flag and claiming the land, like Columbus claiming the 30 New World for Spain. Anyone who seriously breaks this equidistant rule will probably be watched very carefully to try to find out the reason for their unusual action.

4

35 Smaller things like a towel can, of course, be used to reserve a smaller space on the beach, but very importantly it is a much smaller space. It is fascinating to see how long just one towel will successfully reserve a space on a beach. I
40 decided to try this by placing a towel on a beach early one morning and to sit and watch what happened as the beach started to fill up.

5

To begin with, it was an extremely effective territorial marker. In fact, as couples and groups
45 arrived on the beach you could see them taking the position of the towel into account in their calculations of the best sites for themselves. It was treated with equal respect by passers-by as well. On their way to the sea they carefully by-

passed it. One young French boy accidentally 50 stepped on it and was told off by his mother.

6

This unfortunate accident marked the beginning of the end of the territorial marking powers of this particular towel and it was noticeable that thereafter passers-by took less care to avoid it. 55 More and more feet stepped closer and closer, until it was nearly covered in sand. Eventually a middle-aged lady walked right over it. The end of the towel was now turned up and it was immediately apparent that all of its remaining 60 powers had now faded. Shortly after this happened, a young couple sat down in the exact spot marked by the towel, and the young man merely threw the sandy and now dirty towel onto some rocks behind the beach. However, it 65 had managed to reserve this space successfully for nearly three hours!

Responding to the text

1 Read the first paragraph of the text carefully.

Work with another student. Look at this imaginary conversation between a reader of the text and its writer. The reader is trying to summarise the paragraph and then to check the summary with the writer. Take one role each and read the conversation aloud.

Reader: You seem to be criticising people for bringing so much to the beach.
Writer: Not exactly criticising. I'm just describing what I see.
Reader: But you wouldn't carry all those things to the beach with you?
Writer: Perhaps I wouldn't.

2 Read the second paragraph carefully. Still with your partner, continue the conversation between a reader of the text and its writer.

Reader: So you think it's a good idea for people to be well prepared to spend the day on the beach?
Writer: That's not really what I meant.
Reader:
Writer:

3 Read the third paragraph carefully and have another short conversation with your partner. Then try doing the same thing after reading the other paragraphs. Take it in turns to role-play reader and writer and have short conversations about the text.

EXAM TIP 12

In Part 1 of the exam, you will need to get a good summary of each paragraph in order to match it to the correct heading or summary sentence. One way of doing this is to imagine you are talking to the writer: think of intelligent comments to make and then check back in the text to see what the writer's replies would be.

Exam practice: Part 1 Multiple matching

Choose the most suitable heading from the list A–F for each part of the text (1–6). Write the appropriate letter in each numbered gap. Use your 'conversations' about the text to help you.

A A little experiment

B A matter of personal space

C A convincing performance

D Mathematics, conquest and an alert eye

E Power in decline

F A major expedition

Extension

Work with another student. Discuss these questions.

1 Have you had a holiday on the beach? If so, what did you notice about the way people keep themselves apart from others?
2 How much notice did you take of the 'territorial markers' mentioned in the text?
3 Look at the objects below. Where and how could you use them to defend your territory?

Unit 5 How green was my holiday?

Reading skills:	Revising techniques for getting an overall picture
	Analysing the text: reference words
	Dealing with difficult words by using the context
Exam focus:	Part 2 Multiple choice comprehension questions
Theme:	Holidays – see page 112 for a Part 2 practice test on the same theme

Getting an overall picture

1 Look back at Unit 1 (page 10), Unit 3 (page 18) and Unit 4 (page 22) where you practised getting an overall picture from words which occur again and again in a text, from titles and from illustrations.

Now look at the text on the opposite page. You have one minute only to get an overall picture. Use one of the techniques you have practised.

2 Discuss these questions with another student.

1 What does the picture represent?
2 Are there any national parks in your country?
3 Have you ever been to a national park? If so, which one(s)?
4 Do you think there are any problems with national parks? If so, what?

Find out which 'overall picture' technique your partner used. Discuss which techniques would be most useful for this type of text.

Analysing the text

1 Look at the second sentence in the text.

That's certainly how they see themselves.

To understand this sentence you have to read the first sentence too, because the second sentence refers back to it.

That refers to *practical down-to-earth no-nonsense types*
they refers to *Americans*
themselves refers to *they*

As you practised in Unit 3, you can show what reference words refer to like this:

Most people tend to think of Americans as practical down-to-earth no-nonsense types.
That's certainly how they see themselves.

Now look at the last sentence of the first paragraph. Find the reference words *They* and *both*. Use the same method to show what they refer to.

Loved to death

Most people tend to think of Americans as practical down-to-earth no-non-sense types. That's 5 certainly how they see themselves. I suspect however that the opposite is the case. What Americans like most 10 is a good, wide-ranging philosophical argument, plus a crisis. They have invented both for their national parks system.

15 The crisis is that the parks are being, in the popular phrase, 'loved to death'. Too many people are visiting the system – 20 up to almost 400 million last year. It's said they are ruining the plants with the pollution from their cars, scaring the ani- 25 mals, destroying by their numbers the wilderness experience the parks are supposed to offer.

It's hard for a visitor from 30 Europe to feel that way. Three years ago we went to the Grand Tetons in Wyoming which is my favourite park of all. Yes, the car parks were full. Yes, you 35 could find yourself waiting behind a line of cars as someone tried to photograph a herd of animals with a pocket camera.

But then we drove a little 40 way north, turned off the main road and found a small lake surrounded by fields of flowers, with the beautiful snow-capped range of the Tetons in the back- 45 ground. We saw a total of two other people during the whole long, sunny, perfect afternoon.

The busiest park in the system, the Great Smoky 50 Mountains between Tennessee and North Carolina, can get 60,000 visitors on a single summer's day. That sounds plenty and it is, but all of these 55 people are sharing an area only slightly smaller than the whole of Luxembourg, which has a permanent population seven times as great.

60 Of course there are problems. Take Yosemite, the best-known park in California. Yosemite has luxury houses commanding the finest views built for the 65 executives of the company which owns all the park's cafés and restaurants. There's a video rental store now and even a small prison, for visitors who get drunk and 70 disorderly. In spite of this, the main environ-mental threat is smog drifting east from Los Angeles. 75

And so to the philo-sophical question. This takes many forms, but the basic argument is over how much should 80 be done in the parks to satisfy human visitors. Should the accommoda-tion be so basic that only true lovers of nature will 85 be tempted to come? Or should it contain – as it increasingly does – en suite bathrooms and colour TVs? Choose 90 the former and you are necessarily exclud-ing America's growing population of old people, many of them desperate to enjoy a 95 first experience of their own country's beauty.

And exactly what should be preserved? Twenty years ago Yellow Stone, perhaps the most 100 famous park of all, decided to change to a 'hands-off' policy. Animals in danger of starving in the winter would be left to starve, just as nature intended. 105

My advice is to stop trying too hard. Provide plenty of car parks and lodgings for visitors of all kinds. Ban radios and snowmobiles. But realise 110 that for every thousand acres which are spoiled, there are a million which remain as beautiful as they were in George Washington's day. 115

2 Find the following sentences in the text.

  1 It's hard for a visitor from Europe to feel that way. (lines 29–30)
  2 That sounds plenty and it is. (lines 53–54)
  3 In spite of this, the main environmental threat is smog drifting east from Los Angeles. (lines 71–75)
  4 Or should it contain – as it increasingly does – en suite bathrooms and colour TVs? (lines 86–90)

With another student, find the reference words in the sentences and use coloured pencils to show what they refer to.

EXAM TIP 13

In order to read accurately, you often need to analyse words like *this*, *that*, *as*, *how* and pronouns, working out what they refer to. Some multiple choice comprehension questions in Part 2 of the exam explicitly require you to do this.

Dealing with difficult words

Find the following phrases in the text.

the wilderness experience the parks are supposed to offer (lines 26–28)

the beautiful snow-capped range of the Tetons in the background (lines 43–45)

Animals in danger of starving in the winter would be left to starve (lines 103–105)

Look at the context around the phrases and answer these questions.

1 Who are, apparently, destroying the *wilderness experience*?
How are they destroying it?
Bearing in mind how it is being destroyed, what do you think the *wilderness experience* is?
2 What else might you expect to see in a national park, apart from lakes, fields and flowers?
What might you expect to see with snow on it?
What might you expect to see in the background?
So what do you think the *range of the Tetons* is?
3 What is the connection between a *hands-off policy* and *just as nature intended*?
What dangers do animals face in winter?
So what do you think *starve* means?

EXAM TIP 14

You can often guess the meaning of unfamiliar words by looking at the context and by using your own general knowledge. This technique is even more effective if you combine it, where possible, with the technique of breaking words down into parts, which you practised in Unit 4.

Exam practice: Part 2 Multiple choice comprehension questions

Choose the answer which you think fits best according to the text.

1 According to the writer, what have Americans invented?

   A a no-nonsense approach to their national parks
   B an argument and a crisis regarding their national parks
   C an argument which is both wide-ranging and insoluble
   D a system of two national parks

2 What reaction do visitors from Europe have when touring in the parks?

   A The level of pollution makes it difficult for them to feel anything.
   B They have no reaction because it is too hard to get out of the traffic queues and into the wilderness.
   C They have to be tough to accept the destruction of plants and animals.
   D It is difficult for them to sympathise with the view that the parks are being destroyed.

3 What point does the writer make about accommodation in national parks?

   A Providing only basic accommodation would mean that elderly people would not be able to stay in the parks.
   B A growing number of people would not like to stay in accommodation with en suite bathrooms and colour TVs.
   C Accommodation should be basic to ensure that the wrong sort of people stay away from the parks.
   D The accommodation should increasingly contain better facilities.

4 *this* in line 72 refers to damage to the environment caused by

   A cafés and restaurants.
   B a small prison.
   C drunkenness among visitors.
   D the amount of building.

Extension

Discuss these questions with one or two other students.

1 Who visits the countryside in your country: mostly old people, mostly young people, or everyone?
2 Do people in your country enjoy staying in 'basic' accommodation when visiting the countryside? Or do they prefer comfortable hotels?
3 Do you think we should try to preserve nature by stopping people from going to certain areas of the country?
4 Can there be any tourism without pollution and destruction?

Unit 6 A holiday in the Caribbean

Reading skills: Dealing with difficult words by using a combination of techniques

Revising techniques for keeping your purpose in mind and ignoring irrelevant information

Exam focus: Part 4 Multiple matching

Theme: Holidays – see page 100 for a Part 4 practice test on the same theme

The text in this unit is from a brochure for Caribbean holidays.

Dealing with difficult words

1 Look back at Unit 4 (page 23) and Unit 5 (page 28) where you practised how to guess the meaning of unfamiliar words by breaking them down into parts and by using the context.

Now study this sentence. What do you think is the meaning of *overhang*?

> In the main town, wooden balconies overhang the street.

Divide the word into two parts. Try to imagine balconies and the street below. Draw a small sketch to help you. Then use the same technique to work out the meaning of the words in italics in the following sentences.

1 You may dream of *faraway* beautiful beaches.
2 St. Lucia's most famous *landmark* is the twin volcanic cones called the Pitons.
3 Antigua's rocky *coastline* can provide a beach for every day of the year.
4 *Woodland* and waterfalls, history and tradition, sun and sports, Jamaica has it all.
5 The sands of the north coast resorts are bordered with *offshore* coral reefs.

2 Now try to guess the meaning of the words in italics in the following sentences. This time you will need to look for clues in the roots of the words. In each case choose the most suitable suggestion.

1 For centuries the Caribbean has enchanted and *captivated* the traveller.

a) held in prison   b) held the attention of   c) held on ships   d) held very tightly

2 St. Lucia is famous for its scenic *grandeur*, Antigua for its range of beautiful beaches.

a) variety   b) riches   c) beauty   d) magnificence

3 Visitors to the island find the gentle pace, infectious calm and general *contentment* very attractive.

a) happiness   b) restraint   c) countryside   d) ingredients

3 Can you guess the meaning of the words in italics in these sentences without help?

1 The sugar-white sands of Jamaica's north coast resorts are *legendary*.
2 Barbados is as historic as *piracy* on the high seas.
3 On the island there are championship golf courses and *floodlit* tennis courts.

EXAM TIP 15

You can often guess the approximate meaning of new words by 'taking them apart' and analysing the individual parts. Sometimes this is not possible, but you can still guess the meaning by looking at the root of the word. You can increase your chances of success by checking the context too.

Keeping your purpose in mind and ignoring irrelevant information

1 Look at these different interests four holidaymakers to the Caribbean might have.

1 I love shopping at local markets.

2 Sport is my passion – I particularly like playing golf.

3 I never get tired of going to the beach. It's so relaxing.

4 When I'm on holiday, I like to get right away from civilisation.

Work with another student and try to think of a one- or two-word summary to remember each interest by.

2 Read the text on the next page as quickly as you can and highlight or underline words and expressions which correspond to your summaries.

Work with the same partner and compare your texts. Have you marked the same things? Discuss the differences, then answer these questions.

Which island(s) would you recommend for each holidaymaker? Why?

EXAM TIP 16

When you are doing Part 4 of the examination you are required only to extract particular information. You can ignore irrelevant information by looking quickly through the text for specific words or expressions which relate to your reading purpose.

Your beautiful Caribbean holiday

It is said that for every individual dream of faraway sands there is a perfectly matching Caribbean island. For centuries the Caribbean has enchanted and captivated the traveller with the combination of perfect beaches of dazzling white sands, palm trees shaking in the soft winds and a pace of life that is decidedly relaxed. We have selected four of the most
5 popular islands: St. Lucia, Antigua, Jamaica and Barbados.

A | St. Lucia

A mystical island of volcanic mountains, St. Lucia is a charmed and charming place. Its scenic grandeur is second to none: secret bays of deep sand, sky-high mountain sides
10 covered in dense forestry and whole valleys of banana groves make for dramatic scenery and yet they are upstaged for sheer rarity by its most famous landmark – the twin volcanic cones, called the Pitons. With a history as
15 complex as its tropical greenery and perhaps the friendliest people in the Caribbean, it's difficult to know if they are a product of the island or the vital ingredient that makes it what it is. Either way, they welcome the
20 visitor with a refreshing enthusiasm – and a spicy traditional cuisine. St. Lucia is undeveloped (as are its roads and services!) and while it remains unspoilt, it may spoil you for anywhere else.

B | Antigua

25 It's said that Antigua has a beach for every day of the year and its rocky coastline of deep inlets, long peninsulas and natural harbours certainly supports the theory. However, it's a legend that is difficult to prove, for visitors to
30 the island are so quickly intoxicated with the gentle pace, infectious calm and general contentment, that no-one is inclined to do a count. One thing is certain, the coral island of Antigua has the finest shores of pink-white
35 sand in all the Caribbean. Apart from the beach, there is plenty of sightseeing as Antigua's unsophisticated charm is spellbinding. In the capital, St. Johns, wooden balconies a century old overhang the street
40 and the market is a battlefield where gossip is exchanged with goods.

C | Jamaica

As colourful as its history, as lively as its local reggae rhythm, and as scenic as any island you will find, Jamaica's magical magnet draws eager visitors to its shores in ever- 45 increasing numbers. Woodland and waterfalls, history and tradition, sun and sports, modern Jamaica has it all. The sugar-white sands of the north coast resorts are legendary and bordered with offshore coral 50 reefs, providing a wide choice of water-based activity, from snorkelling to jetskiing, scuba diving to parasailing. The landscape too, more than simply beautiful, lends itself to recreation. You can climb the water-smoothed 55 steps of Dunn's River Falls, play golf on a number of world class courses, go rafting on the Rio Grande. So much more than sun and sand, Jamaica is the Caribbean encapsulated, a rich reserve of holiday experiences. 60

D | Barbados

As British as cricket and afternoon tea, as historic as piracy on the high seas, as exotic as calypso and coral reefs, as Caribbean as you could wish, Barbados is a matchless mix of sunshine, sport and sophistication. The 65 sunniest in a sea of tropical treasures, Barbados is blessed with beautiful beaches, where, centuries ago, smugglers and pirates used to land. The fashionable west coast is caressed by the cool Caribbean, while the 70 eastern shoreline is battered by the crashing Atlantic surf. Those who enjoy land sports are well looked after, with championship golf and floodlit tennis courts and on warm Barbados evenings the 'millionaires' playground' of the 75 West Indies comes alive with the characteristic music of steel bands, the cool sound of jazz and the more relaxed Latin American rhythms. Yet the island preserves a certain charm, gentility and sophistication, in 80 classical colonial plantation mansions, in old-world values of courtesy and dress code and the time-honoured tradition of taking life slowly, so it lasts longer … Decide that 'rushing' is just something they make baskets 85 from and you're well on the way to discovering the Barbados spirit.

Exam practice: Part 4 Multiple matching

Answer questions 1–10 by choosing from the Caribbean islands (A–D) in the text. The islands may be chosen more than once. When more than one answer is required, these may be given in any order.

Which island(s) would you recommend for a holidaymaker who

is particularly interested in traditional old buildings?	**1**	**2**	
enjoys different kinds of music?		**3**	
enjoys eating peppery food?		**4**	
wants to meet the local population?		**5**	
wants to do a lot of watersports?		**6**	
likes a relaxed pace of life?	**7**	**8**	
likes spectacular landscapes?	**9**	**10**	

Extension

Work with another student and discuss these questions.

1 If you could choose to go on holiday anywhere in the world, where would you go, and why?
2 What are the most important factors when choosing a holiday? Put the following in order of importance.

Beautiful scenery   Good entertainment
History and culture   A variety of different beaches
Sports facilities   Relaxing lifestyle
Friendly people   Good food and good shopping

Unit 7 The lion cub

Getting an overall picture

1 Read the text on the opposite page as far as the word *come* (line 8).

Work with another student. Summarise the beginning of the story, using these phrases. Put them in the correct order to make two or three sentences.

> with a lion cub   a few weeks later   one day   I went with Maurice
> he looked very proud   to see the same lion cub   a man came into the surgery
> to the zoo

2 Discuss these questions with another student.

1 Which of these jobs do you think is Maurice's?

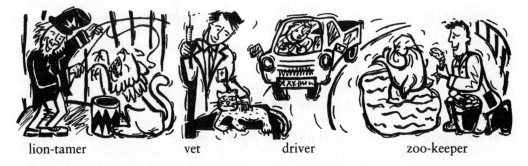

lion-tamer   vet   driver   zoo-keeper

2 Why do you think the man brought the cub to the surgery?
3 Why was Maurice astonished?
4 Why was the man proud?
5 Why do you think the cub is now in a zoo?

EXAM TIP 17

Sometimes you can get a good overall picture just by reading the first few lines of a text. This is because some writers like to give you an idea from the beginning of how the story might end.

34

The lion cub

'It's my morning at the zoo,' said Maurice, 'would you like to come? We'll have a look at that lion cub and see how he's getting on in his new surroundings.'

'You mean the one that was brought into the surgery a few weeks ago?'

'Yes.'

5   I settled myself in the car and, as we drove away, I thought back to a morning when a man had come in with a lion cub pulling on a heavy chain. Smiling proudly at our astonished faces, he said, 'Grand little chap, isn't he? Only twelve weeks old and tough as they come. I got him through an advertisement in the newspaper. My little girl is delighted and simply loves him but he's a bit rough
10 when he gets excited. He'll be safer for her to play with when you've dealt with him.' ✶1

I looked up in surprise and Maurice asked, 'What do you mean by "dealt with him"?'

'Well, when you've filed down his teeth and taken out his claws.' Picking up
15 the cub, the man held him out to Maurice. 'The people I bought him from said this was the thing to do.'

'They did, did they?' Maurice's face was solemn as he rubbed the little animal under the chin. 'And how long will you keep him? Nine months? A year?' ✶2

'Oh, when he gets too big for us he'll have to go into a zoo. But we'll give him a
20 good time while he's little and then, of course, he'll want to be with his own kind. We'll visit him regularly, though. We're great animal lovers, you understand.' ✶3

Maurice nodded, put the cub on the floor, pulled up a chair for the man and sat down himself. 'I think,' he said, 'that you have been misled. I wouldn't dream of hurting a wild animal like that and I don't know any other vet who would do
25 it either. You say you will give him to a zoo when he gets too big but with no claws he couldn't be put in with other lions – he'd have no means of self-defence and he'd be killed. So he would have to be kept on his own. So he wouldn't have much of a life, would he? In fact, it would be very difficult to find a zoo – a good one anyway – that would take him.' ✶4

30 The man shook his head. 'I never thought of it like that.' He paused, then, bending down, he pushed the cub away from his chair.

There was a tiny roar, the cub's lips curled back and he stared up with
35 angry eyes. His owner lifted him and held him tightly in his arms. Then he said helplessly, 'But what on earth am I to do
40 with him? What do you advise?' ✶5

'He obviously can't play with your little daughter,' said Maurice. 'He's quite fierce already. And it won't be easy to get a zoo to take him. Most of them have enough cubs as it is. They're almost two a penny, but, if you like …'
45   'Two a penny? Good God! I paid a hundred pounds for him!'
There was a long silence. 'So I've been "done" have I?' The man stared down at his cub. *6
Maurice nodded. 'I'm afraid so. Unfortunately there are lots of dishonest people about who are profiting from this fashion for exotic pets.' *7
50   The man frowned. 'Exotic pets? Well, yes, I suppose you're right. It's rather nice to cause a bit of a sensation with something out of the ordinary.'
'If you like,' said Maurice slowly, 'I'll ask the manager of our local zoo if he can fit this little one in with some cubs who are being raised on the bottle. They're roughly the same age and he would probably be accepted.' *8
55   And so it turned out.

Responding to the text

Work with another student. Read the text from the beginning and think about the characters of the two men in the story. Each time you see the sign *, stop reading and choose a word from the chart below to describe the speaker at that point. Make sure you can find phrases in the text to support your choice. One example has been done for you.

Maurice	*	*Supporting phrase*
worried	....	....
severe	....	....
businesslike	....	....
sympathetic	....	....

Man with cub		
proud	...*1*....	*Only twelve weeks old and tough as they come* ....
enthusiastic	....	....
confused	....	....
shocked	....	....

EXAM TIP 18

When reading fiction, a good way to respond to the text is to try to form an opinion of the characters in the story.

Analysing the text

Look carefully again at lines 22–29 of the text. Discuss these questions with another student.

1 What does *like that* (line 24) refer to?
2 Where could you fit the following words and phrases into lines 25–27?

   a) if he went to a zoo   b) because   c) so

EXAM TIP 19

Very often parts of a text are connected to each other without special linking words like *because* or *so*. When this happens, think carefully about the logical connection of the ideas and try to put your own linking words into the text.

And if so, then however!

Exam practice: Part 2 Multiple choice comprehension questions

Choose the answer which you think fits best according to the text.

1 Why did Maurice go to the zoo?

   A to see the lion cub
   B he wanted to take his friend
   C to see the new surroundings
   D he had work to do there

2 Why did Maurice refuse to take out the cub's claws?

   A The man wanted to give it to a zoo.
   B It could not protect itself against other lions.
   C He didn't know how to do it.
   D It was too small to have its claws removed.

3 Why did Maurice think it would be hard to find a zoo that would take the cub?

   A The cub was too aggressive.
   B Most zoos are overcrowded.
   C Most zoos don't need more lion cubs.
   D The cub was not worth very much.

4 The man was shocked and said 'Good God!' because

   A he had thought he would easily be able to find a zoo.
   B Maurice had discovered his real reasons for buying the lion.
   C he realised he had been tricked into paying too much for the lion.
   D Maurice had explained that his daughter wouldn't be able to play with the lion.

Extension

Discuss these questions with another student.

1 Why do you think people keep pets?
2 Have you got any pets? If not, what sort of pet would you like?
3 What is the best animal to have as a pet? Why?
4 Do you think animals like being kept as pets? Why/why not?

Unit 8 Zooooooh!

Reading skills:	Getting an overall picture by reading the first and last paragraphs and thinking about the text type and style
	Analysing the text: participles
Exam focus:	Part 3 Gapped text
Theme:	Animals – see page 114 for a Part 3 practice test on the same theme

Getting an overall picture

1 Look at the title of the text on page 40. Discuss these questions with another student.

   1 What are the arguments in favour of zoos?
   2 What are the arguments against them?
   3 Why do you think the word *zoo* has been spelt in this way?
      (Try saying the title in the way it has been spelt!)

Now quickly read the first and the last paragraphs of the text. Discuss these questions with your partner.

Do you think the writer is in favour of zoos or against them? Why?

2 Think about the title and the two paragraphs you have read. Do you think this article appeared in a popular magazine for general readers? Or did it appear in a specialist magazine for, say, university researchers?

Work with another student. Read the pairs of sentences in the chart on the opposite page. Decide which sentence in each pair comes from a popular magazine and which from a specialist magazine.

Sentence A	*Sentence B*
1 What is the reason for maintaining caged animals?	Why is a tiger lying in a cage?
2 There's just nothing like the experience of coming face to face with real, live, wild animals.	The experience of meeting live, wild animals cannot be replaced.
3 The image of wild animals is falsified by even the best of zoos.	The zoo – good, bad, best in the world – presents a false picture of wild animals.
4 We should be mainly concerned with animals, not zoo visitors.	Start with the animals, not the people.

Now read the text carefully. While you are reading, check which sentence from each pair is in the article.

EXAM TIP 20

Another good way to get an overall picture of a text before reading thoroughly is to look at the first and last paragraphs and use them to think about the content and style of the text. Ask yourself questions about the type of text it is and about the style of the writer's message. Will it contain a lot of sentences in the passive? Are there likely to be many phrasal verbs? Will the sentences be long or short?

Analysing the text

1 Look at the two sentences below.

1 Having tried to play several different musical instruments, <u>I</u> understand how difficult it can be.
2 Constructed back in the eighteenth century, <u>the house</u> was completely modernised twenty years ago.

The underlined word in each sentence is the subject. The *-ing* participle at the beginning of the first sentence and the *-ed* participle at the beginning of the second shows that there are two actions in each sentence, one following the other. To clarify the meaning of the two sentences, you could rewrite them, starting with the subject and using a linking word to connect the ideas.

1 I have tried to play several different musical instruments *so* I understand how difficult it can be.
2 The house was constructed back in the eighteenth century *and* was completely modernised twenty years ago.

Zooooooh!

'Look! He's waving at you!
Wave wave. Say "hello".
Look at his tail, he's waving
at you ...'
5   'Not very fierce, is he?
Come on then, show us your
teeth ...'
   'He would make a nice
rug, wouldn't he?'
10   The tiger lies on the
concrete floor, staring into
space. People stop, make
remarks, then go – having
taken their photos, made
15 their jokes and had their
'good day out'.
   But wait a minute. This is
the millennium. [1]
Why is a tiger lying in a cage
20 in this day and age?
   It depends on where you
are standing. From inside the
zoo director's office, for
example, the tiger is living
25 very comfortably. [2]
I have heard one zoo director
describe the zoo as a 'welfare
state' for animals.
   But the zoo director also
30 tells us that the tiger is
earning its keep by educating
the public. [3]   The
argument goes like this: all
the nature and wildlife
35 documentary films in the
world can't replace flesh and
blood. There's just nothing
like the experience of coming
face to face with real, live,
40 wild animals. [4]
Along with all the other
caged animals, the tiger – to
use a favourite zoo phrase –
is an 'ambassador for the
45 wild'.

As someone who studies
human behaviour, I'm
interested in why people go
to zoos, what they get from
50 looking at animals in cages
and what zoos say they
get. [5]   No zoo can
bring about a meaningful
meeting between people and
55 animals because by its very
nature the zoo – good, bad,
best in the world – presents a
false picture of wild animals
and our relationship with
60 them. Zoos are for people,
not animals.
   The time I have spent
outside the cages has showed
me how the zoo hinders any
65 true understanding of
animals. [6]   With
their painted scenery, zoos
are like theatres – and the

relationship they set up
70 between visitors and animals
is that of audience and
performers.
   The only way we can bring
about any healthy and
75 relaxed meeting between
people and imprisoned
animals is to do away with
the idea of zoos and to start
again. Start with the animals,
80 not the people. [7]
Find ways of offering them
somewhere which can
realistically replace the wild,
an imaginative space of the
85 right size, a chance to relate
to other animals as they
would in the wild, a chance
to get away from the public
stares – a chance, basically, to
90 live their own lives.

2 The sentences below have been taken out of the text. Underline the participle and the subject of each sentence. Then rewrite each sentence, starting with the subject and using a linking word to connect the ideas.

A Having seen wild animals close up, zoo visitors will be so enthusiastic about the wonders of the natural world that they will start to care deeply about what is happening to wild animals, go off and do something about it.

B Robbed of all its natural grace, the animal is shut into a space which is designed and controlled by people.

C Saved from having to earn its own living in the tough outside world, it has all its meals provided and doesn't even have to walk anywhere.

D Having spent hours watching people watching animals, I don't believe that any zoo can fulfil the high-minded educational aim it says it has.

EXAM TIP 21

When doing Part 3 of the exam, you can help yourself to understand sentences taken from the text by rephrasing them. Analyse sentences beginning with participles particularly carefully. This can make it easier to find their correct place in the text.

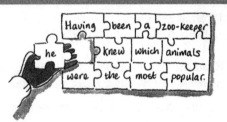

Exam practice: Part 3 Gapped text

Choose from the sentences A–D above and E–H below the one which fits each numbered gap (1–7) in the text. There is one extra sentence which you do not need to use. Use your text analysis skills to help you.

E Ask what reasons there could be for ever keeping them in cages.

F When their existence is put into question zoos always answer by saying that they educate people.

G They are protected in zoos because they will not survive in the wild.

H We've all turned green and are trying to save rain forests.

Extension

Discuss these questions with another student.

1 What do you think are the alternatives to zoos?
2 Do you agree with the writer that it is wrong to want to be entertained by animals?
3 Apart from entertainment and education, are there any other reasons for keeping wild animals in captivity?
4 Zoos are closing down in many cities because people no longer go to them. Why do you think this is?

Unit 9 A different point of view

> *Reading skills:* Getting an overall picture by using a combination of techniques
> Responding to the text by paraphrasing while you read
> Analysing the text: linking words
> *Exam focus:* Part 1 Multiple matching
> *Theme:* Animals – see page 86 for a Part 1 practice test on the same theme

Getting an overall picture

1 Look at the title of the text on the opposite page. Discuss these questions with another student.

   1 What are you an owner of?
   2 Who could *your owner* be?

2 Read the first sentence of each paragraph. Then look quickly through the rest of the text to see if any words appear again and again.

Discuss these questions with another student.

   1 Who is the owner in the title?
   2 Which kind of very special (and unusual!) reader is the text supposed to be written for?
   3 Who do you think the text is really written for?
   4 What is the purpose of the text, do you think?
   5 What sort of suggestions or advice do you think it will give concerning understanding owners?

EXAM TIP 22

You can combine many different approaches to get an overall picture. Always remember to spend some time thinking about the text and getting an overall picture before you start reading carefully. You can do this by looking at words which occur again and again, by thinking about the title and illustration(s), by reading the first few lines or the first and last paragraphs, and by thinking about the text type and style.

Understanding your owner

1 ☐

Although I know that many of you think the opposite, most human beings have a high level of intelligence, a good memory and can solve a great deal of problems. They live longer and therefore tend to be much more aware of past and future than we are.

2 ☐

Humans communicate by a set of sounds which carry meaning from the order in which they
5 are placed, and which vary from territory to territory, so that some humans find difficulty in communicating with others according to where they come from – if they have been raised in a different country and have not had special training. They have also invented a set of marks on paper which they use to represent these sounds and which you may often see them concentrating on. In these two ways they have developed their eyes and ears to a higher level
10 of interpretation than ourselves, but in doing so they have lost the ability to gather much of the information which we continually do both from these and our other senses.

3 ☐

Most dogs are able to interpret at least part of the vocabulary (voice meanings) of humans, and some of us have learned to recognise some of the pattern of marks which they use to record them on paper so that humans at a different time and in a different place can
15 understand their messages, but it would put our other abilities into danger if we ourselves developed these skills very far. Fortunately, most humans are able to understand a similar amount of our communicatory sounds and behaviour.

4 ☐

Try going up to a human, sitting down in front of him and raising a front paw in a gesture. He will almost certainly take it and give it a shake, because it is a greeting gesture for
20 humans, too. He will think you are behaving like a human – and nothing seems to please humans more.

5 ☐

Careful, there is a danger here! You are not a human. You are a dog – and if you are going to be at all happy you should never forget it. You need to live as a dog. It is all very well changing yourself slightly to fit in with a human pack, but if you deny your true nature you
25 are going to end up a mad dog and, humans will think, a bad dog.

6 ☐

There is always a reason for any animal choosing to live with an animal of a different sort, but all too often we have no choice. We have to live with humans and we have to join a pack that is forced on us, so there is not much you can do about it. But humans have consciously decided that they want us with them, although not necessarily for the reason that they believe.
30 They may need a dog to help with some specific task like hunting or guiding. They may want you as a watchdog to keep burglars away. They may have some idea that looking after you will teach their pups a sense of responsibility. They may just want you to make other humans look at them, because your breed is expensive and fashionable. Or they may simply be in desperate need of companionship, of something to love.

Responding to the text

Read the text carefully. As you read, try to find words and phrases in the text which mean the same as the words and phrases below (you will find them in the same order in the text).

imagine	reading
cleverness	the noises dogs make
language	a sign which means 'hello'
place	to manage to live with people
brought up	to give up
a language course at school	real identity

When you have finished reading, compare your synonyms with another student. See if you have found the same phrases.

EXAM TIP 23

Remember that a good way to read efficiently is to try to rephrase parts of the text in your own words while you are reading. In Part 1 of the exam, the headings and summary sentences you have to match to the sections of the text often contain synonyms of words or phrases you have read.

Analysing the text

1 Work with another student. Find the following words and phrases in the text and choose the appropriate definition from the list.

1 therefore (line 3)

   a) despite this   b) as a result of this   c) also

2 in doing so (line 10)

   a) in spite of this   b) in order to do this   c) because of this

3 if you are going to be at all happy (lines 22–23)

   a) assuming you want to be happy   b) imagining you will be happy
   c) on condition that you are happy

2 Say which sentence in each pair is true, according to the text.

1 a) Humans tend to be more aware of past and future because they live longer.
   b) Humans tend to live longer because they are more aware of past and future.

2 a) Humans have lost their information-gathering ability because they have developed their eyes and ears to a high level.
   b) Humans have been able to develop their eyes and ears to a high level because they have lost their information-gathering ability.

3 a) If dogs are happy they will never lose their identity.
   b) If dogs do not lose their identity they will be happy.

EXAM TIP 24

Pay special attention to linking words and phrases. If you misunderstand them, you will risk misunderstanding the whole text.

Exam practice: Part 1 Multiple matching

Choose the most suitable heading from the list A–G for each part (1–6) of the article. There is one extra heading which you do not need to use. Use the synonyms you studied on page 44 and your text analysis skills to help you.

> A How human language works
>
> B How language fits the place
>
> C Cleverer than you imagine
>
> D A level of communication
>
> E A matter of choice?
>
> F Avoiding an identity crisis
>
> G A sign in common

Extension

Discuss these questions with one or two students.

1 Can you think of any other gestures, apart from shaking hands, which both dogs and humans perform?
2 What advice does this text give to dog owners?
3 What advice could you give to another kind of pet about living with humans?
4 What do you think animals gain, and what do they lose, from living with humans?

Unit 10 How to get a laugh

Getting an overall picture

1 The title of the text in this unit (on page 48) is *How to get a laugh*.

Work with another student.

Student A: Close your book.
Student B: Read this short story aloud. Does your partner laugh?

> A lady went into a hotel. The receptionist was reading a newspaper. In front of the reception
> desk there was a pretty little dog. The lady wanted to stroke it.
>   'Does your dog bite?' she said to the receptionist.
>   'No,' said the receptionist, hardly looking up from his reading.
>   The lady went to pat the dog on the head and it bit her hand. 'I thought you said your dog
> didn't bite!'
>   'It's not my dog,' replied the receptionist.

Now try this 'one-liner'. Any laughs?

> A man was left in the desert with no food. How did he live? Because of the sandwiches there
> (the sand which is there).

**Discuss the kinds of things that make you laugh – jokes, one-liners, TV programmes,
things that happen to members of your family.**

2 The subtitle says that the text will give away secrets. The first line of the text introduces
the joke writer, Gene Perret. Look over the text for one minute. Look for the name *Perret*
and try to find some of the secrets he gives away.

46

Work with another student. Make a list of the secrets Perret gives away. Try to think of a practical example of each secret.

EXAM TIP 25

Always try to imagine what the text is about before reading intensively. This will make your reading more efficient. Use the information in titles and subtitles to help you.

Responding to the text

Work with another student who reads at about the same speed as you. Read the text carefully. At the end of paragraphs 2, 4, 6 and 7, stop reading and summarise in your own words the main ideas in the paragraph(s) you have read. See if you both agree.

When you have finished reading the whole text choose from the list the summary which is closest to yours.

Paragraphs 1–2
  a) Humour has an important role to play in communication, and is available to everyone, as the story about the air steward showed.
  b) Humour can save lives, which is why the air steward told jokes.
  c) Humour stops you from making a serious point – the air steward's jokes would not save lives.

Paragraphs 3–4
  a) Find a collection of funny material, match it to the right people and then try to use humour in your own family.
  b) You need only 25 jokes to start; the rest of your humour should be stories or one-liners from your experience.
  c) After deciding which sort of humour suits you, keep on the lookout for humour, particularly in your own experience.

Paragraphs 5–6
  a) Humour should suit the listeners and you should not appear to attack them.
  b) Audiences like jokes about themselves, as the McDonald's and copying machine stories show.
  c) Be careful when speaking before managers: some of them may enjoy humour while others feel insulted.

Paragraph 7
  a) Open and close speeches with a joke and make sure the entire speech has a strong point.
  b) Don't follow all the rules of making speeches and use jokes to say something important.
  c) Don't forget to use strong jokes in speeches, especially before messages.

Now work with a different partner. Discuss the summary sentences you have chosen. Say why you think your sentences are correct and why the other two sentences cannot be correct in each case.

How to get a laugh

A joke writer gives away the secrets of being funny

1

G ene Perret has been a joke writer for 20 years and has taken hundreds of flights. So he was only half listening when the air steward began going over the
5 safety instructions. Suddenly Perret's ears stood up. 'There may be 50 ways to leave your lover,' the steward said, 'but there are only five ways to leave this aeroplane.' And then: 'Please return your seat to its upright and most uncomfortable
10 position. Later you may lean back and break the knees of the passenger behind you.'

2

Perret uses the air steward story to make a serious point: humour can catch someone's attention and get a message across. 'Some
15 people can't tell a joke to save their lives,' says Perret, 'but everyone can learn to use humour effectively.' The secret is developing your own style, learning a few tricks and taking the time to practise.

3

20 The first step Perret recommends is to build up a 'comedy collection'. Note down 25 jokes or stories that you find funny. Then work out whether you are better with stories or one-liners. Don't try to be what you're not. Matching
25 people with the wrong material is 'like teaching a pig to sing', Perret says. 'It not only wastes your time, it annoys the pig.'

4

Look out for humour on a regular basis, not just before you intend to use it. Joke books are OK, but Perret suggests looking for material from 30 your own experience. He tells a story about helping his little daughter prepare to perform a poem at her school. When he offered to write one for her, she said, 'No, Dad, this is in front of the whole school. I'd rather it was good.' 35 Nothing makes people feel more comfortable than self-critical humour.

5

Material should also fit the audience. When Perret spoke to a meeting of managers of fast-food restaurants, he used this line: 'McDonald's 40 has sold more than 75 billion hamburgers. They know that because they're on their fourth kilo of meat.' It went down well. 'The more humour fits a particular situation, the funnier it is,' Perret says. 45

6

Be careful with insulting humour. Once at a company party, Perret based a whole series of jokes on a copying machine that never worked. In the middle of the speech, the manager of the department stormed out. Now Perret uses as 50 material only matters that audiences joke about themselves.

7

Perret advises people to forget the idea that a
55 speech should open and close with a joke.
Sticking to rules like that could mean insecurity.
If you still insist on a laugh before getting into
your talk, remember that an opening joke or
story must have a strong point that will set up
the entire speech. To give strength to your
60 message, put the joke after it. For instance, one
executive told his employees he wanted them to
attack their most important problems first. He
emphasised the point, saying: 'If you have an
insect to swallow don't look at it too long.' If you
feel you need to end your talk with a joke, make 65
sure you go out with a bang. When a closing
joke falls flat, it is almost impossible to recover.

EXAM TIP 26

In Part 1 of the exam, try to summarise paragraphs yourself before looking back at
the suggested headings or summary sentences. You should have a clear idea of what
the text is about before choosing the appropriate answers.

Exam practice: Part 1 Multiple matching

Choose the most suitable heading from the list A–H for each part (1–7) of the article. There
is one extra heading which you do not need to use. Use your paragraph summaries from
page 47 to help you.

A Your life as a source
B Jokes catch people's attention
C Do what suits you
D A good match
E A tool for everyone
F Attacking doesn't work
G Difficult situations
H Jokes in public speaking

Extension

The text makes the point that humour and laughter help us deal with difficulties. Discuss
these questions with another student.

1 Can you think of any situations where something has been made easier by humour? Or
   where something could have been made easier by humour?
2 Can you think of any situations when you would not like someone to try to be funny?

Unit 11 Superstar

Getting an overall picture

1 **How much do you know about Madonna? Try to complete this paragraph.**

Madonna was an international .... in the 80s and early 90s. Although she was mostly famous for .... , she also .... and wrote .... It is less well-known that she was a .... and can play three ....

2 **Work with another student. Try to complete the 'word spider' below to build up a 'word picture' of Madonna. Use the list of words in the box. You can use some of the words more than once: for example *rhythm* is important in both dancing and songwriting.**

videos   voice   lyric   rhythm   drums   band   studios   choreography   sound
albums   piano   guitar   keep fit

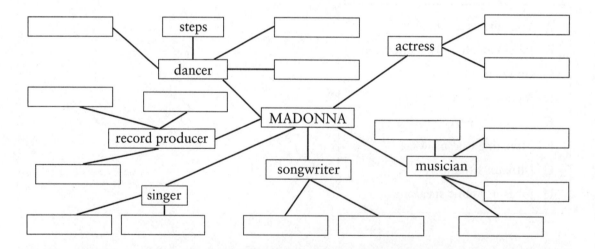

Responding to the text

Imagine the text is a script for a
TV documentary about Madonna.
The pictures on the right are some
scenes for the documentary.
Read the text thoroughly and,
while reading, choose which
scenes should go with the text
and where they should be used.

Work with another student.
Discuss the scenes you have
chosen.

Madonna – Superstar

What is it about Madonna that made her such a trans-continental superstar? The
answer to this question is as varied and covers as wide a range of factors as the subject
herself. At the peak of her career she once said, 'Sometimes I get this scary feeling that
I could do anything I wanted.'

5   She has an exceptional range of creative talents and has achieved success in several
different fields – as a dancer, a singer, a songwriter, a choreographer, a record producer,
a 'tour' artist and an actress.

Madonna trained as a dancer. She really trained, for years, and it was her dancing
skills which brought her to New York in the first place. This was no 'disco-queen',

10 picking up a few steps at the local keep-fit class; her teachers were true professionals,
some of them – Pearl Lang especially – at the summit of their careers. To be a successful
dancer, one has to have a number of skills, but the prime one has to be a sense of
musical rhythm. All successful dancers are musical, and Madonna's years of dance
training have contributed greatly to her success. They gave her a professional approach

15 to choreography, and therefore the making of videos, and enabled her to dance to a high
standard – when she was given the chance – as well as sing. There can be no doubt that
the physical daily discipline of dance training stood her in excellent stead when touring

and spending whole days working in studios without a break, until she had achieved the sound she wanted.

20 She spent almost a year learning how to play drums, the piano and the guitar, adding to her musical skills, and playing in a working band, so that by the time she stood before a band as a singer she could do everything being done by any other member of the band behind her. Her training was therefore complete, but the actual timbre, the quality of her voice, was not to everyone's taste.

25 As a singer, Madonna soon took to writing her own material and her talent as a songwriter has also to be considered. Since she knew her own voice, and she knew the importance of rhythm and syncopation from her dancing, she was able to write songs that were both distinctive and tailor-made for her abilities. Based originally on dance-styles, her songs grew in depth and expressive seriousness so that on the one
30 hand she is responsible for such classics as 'Into The Groove' and on the other she was able to create something as utterly different as 'Promise To Try'. Of course, by no means all of Madonna's songs are entirely her own work; she often writes in collaboration with others but such is her control over all aspects of the finished result that we can justly talk of 'her' material.

35 If her music developed, so did her lyric-writing. Whatever lies behind her lines, some have become phrases within most people's vocabulary; on the *Like A Prayer* album her lyrics rose to new levels of subtlety and literacy.

Analysing the text

Most of the text talks about what Madonna has achieved and how she has achieved it.

1 Explain each achievement (the *what*) with the means (the *how*), using information from the text. One example has been done for you.

Achievements (what she has done)	Means (how she has done it)
1 She has achieved success as a dancer.	*She trained as a dancer.*
2 She dances to a high standard.	
3 She is a good video-maker.	
4 She has written distinctive songs.	
5 She has a professional approach to choreography.	
6 She can spend days working in the studios without a break.	

2 Read the text again. Find these expressions. One of them is followed by a means. Which one is it? (The others are followed by achievements.)

To be (line 11)
contributed to (line 14)
They gave her (line 14)

stood her in excellent stead when (line 17)
so that (line 21)
Since (line 26)

EXAM TIP 29

In order to understand a text fully, you need to be able to make logical connections from one part to another. The multiple choice comprehension questions in Part 2 of the exam often focus on your ability to do this.

Exam practice: Part 2 Multiple choice comprehension questions

Choose the answer which you think fits best according to the text.

1 What does the author say about Madonna's dance training?

   A Her early training was in New York.
   B She learned to dance in a keep-fit class.
   C Her training was thorough and properly supervised.
   D Some of her teachers were professionals.

2 What was the result of Madonna's dance training?

   A It gave her a sense of musical rhythm.
   B It gave her the chance to make dance videos.
   C It helped her to be successful in different areas.
   D It helped her to be independent when she went on tour.

3 How does the author explain Madonna's ability to write songs?

   A She drew on her dance training and a knowledge of her own voice.
   B She had the support and collaboration of others.
   C She had learned to play several musical instruments.
   D She is talented, distinctive and serious.

4 What does the author say about the way Madonna's songs are written?

   A They are all her own work from start to finish.
   B Madonna writes a lot of material herself and is involved in her co-writers' work.
   C The songs are based on dance rhythms and classical themes.
   D She is responsible for the classic songs but not for the others.

Extension

Discuss these questions with another student.

1 What was the secret of Madonna's success? Was it just a matter of working very hard? Do you think you can be successful without working very hard?
2 Do you think Madonna will be remembered in the future? If so, what do you think she will be remembered for?
3 Who are the most famous female singers now? How do they compare with Madonna? Think about their other abilities and talents.

Unit 12 Success in a man's world

Reading skills: Getting an overall picture from capitalised words

Responding to the text by analysing the writer's intentions

Analysing the text: verb tenses and reference words

Exam focus: Part 3 Gapped text

Theme: Success – see page 82 for a Part 3 practice test on the same theme

Getting an overall picture

1 Look at this picture of a professional footballer. What is unusual about the footballer?

2 Work with another student. Look at these words and decide which two words are not about football.

game	championship	medals
kick	racket	league	goal
score	ball	team	rules
pedal	squad		

3 Look through the text *The wild Rose of Trani* as quickly as you can and try to find any words beginning with a capital letter. These will be names of people, places and languages.

Now close your book and write down as many names as you can remember. Compare your names with your partner to make a longer list. Then use your list of names to complete the sentences below. You will find that there are often several grammatically correct possibilities. Write what you think is the most likely or logical.

1 .... is a famous footballer who lives in .... , a town in ....

2 She was born in .... , which is in ....

3 She participated in the .... in .... , the capital of ....

4 Because she was born in .... , she speaks .... , but, living in .... , she also speaks ....

EXAM TIP 30

If a text in the exam contains a lot of different names, you can often get a good overall picture by looking at all the words with capital letters before you start reading intensively.

THE WILD ROSE OF TRANI

JEAN RAFFERTY kicks around a few questions with the girl who's become a star in what is considered a man's
5 **world.**

Rose Reilly comes forward, an elegant creature with sunfrosted hair and a deep tan. Her striped shades of grey and her gold and silver gilt jewellery are unmistakably Italian,
10 indisputably stylish. Is this really what a woman footballer should look like?

1 ⬚

She has lived most of her adult life alone, abroad; first France, then Italy, where the words woman and footballer are not
15 considered a contradiction in terms. In Italy women's football has not only status but audiences in the thousands. A player like Rose, who has more championship medals than anyone else in the women's league and is
20 generally the top goal scorer, earns a substantial salary plus her own apartment and sundry presents from admirers.

2 ⬚

Rose Reilly knows the answers to these questions, because football has always been
25 her life. This is a strange thing for a woman to give her life to. Not because women can't play football. They can.

3 ⬚

She can't explain why she did. She thinks it was something she was born with. There was

never any question of choice for her. While her 30 twin sister Mary played with dolls she was out kicking a ball around with the boys. 'We lived in the streets,' she recalls. 'Stewarton's a wee quiet village in Scotland and there weren't many cars then. It was a different kind of life 35 in those days. You'd go in for bread and jam and then straight back out.

4 ⬚

By 16 Rose was not only a footballer but an athlete of great potential, a member of Scotland's squad for the Commonwealth 40 Games in Edinburgh. That was when she was warned that if she carried on playing football her legs would become too big and muscled for her athletics.

5 ⬚

Later the *Daily Record* flew her out to France, 45 where she joined her first professional team. 'Before then I didn't know women's professional football existed,' she says. Before then she'd had only odd jobs in factories, none of which lasted longer 50 than a week because she hated the feeling of being closed in.

6 ⬚

'But then I made a big decision not to go back home. I took every day as it came and didn't plan anything for the future. Perhaps it was 55 too easy to go back home.' Now after ten years in Italy she speaks English with an Italian intonation and frequently has to search for words in English. She has made Italy her home. 60

Responding to the text

Read through the text slowly and, while you are reading, think about the writer's intentions.

What is the overall 'feel' of the article? Which of these do you think it is?

a) an article to help young footballers develop their professionalism
b) a human interest story about someone a little unusual
c) an amusing article to make you laugh

EXAM TIP 31

Respond to texts by asking yourself who they were written for and what the writer's intentions were.

Analysing the text

The numbered gaps in the text each represent a missing paragraph.

1 Look at the first few paragraphs of the text (lines 6–27). What do you notice about the verb forms in these paragraphs, compared with the verb forms in the rest of the text?

Which verb forms would you expect to find in the first two missing paragraphs?

2 Find these two sentences in the first part of the text. Circle the reference words in each sentence.

> Rose Reilly knows the answers to these questions (lines 23–24)
> She can't explain why she did (line 28)

What do you think missing paragraphs 2 and 3 will be about?

EXAM TIP 32

In Part 3 of the exam, you can often use verb tenses to help you to fit paragraphs and sentences into the gapped texts. A large number of newspaper or magazine articles start with present tenses (including the present perfect) and then go on to use past tenses. Looking carefully at reference words will also help you decide where to put the missing paragraphs or sentences.

Exam practice: Part 3 Gapped text

Choose from the paragraphs A–G below the one which fits each gap (1–6) in the text. There is one extra paragraph which you do not need to use. Use your text analysis skills to help you.

A In a country which is possibly even more football daft than her native Scotland, 30-year-old Rose is a celebrity. She's always being interviewed on TV, usually about why she likes Italy and what her boyfriend thinks about her playing football and what the men think of her legs. Sometimes they even ignore the fact she's a woman and ask her questions about football.

B 'I tried for a week to stop football,' she says, 'but I was used to playing three games a day. I felt like I was sick, as if there was something wrong. I decided to go for the football rather than the athletics even though then there was nothing for women.'

C 'I played with the local boys' team till I was about 12. The opposition never knew I was a girl because I had short hair and I was very young. It was against the rules for a girl to play in the league but they didn't know. I played for a women's team, Stewarton Thistle, after that. I was 12 playing with adult women. They really weren't that good.'

D Rose Reilly's is the story of an obsession. Since the age of four, when she used to take a football to bed with her, the game has been her passion.

E One of the hardest things Rose feels she's been up against is the view that football is a man's world. 'It's incredible how hostile some people are to the idea of women's football,' she says sadly.

F From France she transferred to Italy, to the Trani club. With Rose in the squad, Trani won the championship three years running and were also top of the league. 'It was very strange to me at first,' remembers Rose. 'I was in Italy and I was alone. I lived in a hotel and I used to go to the restaurant twice a day to eat alone. I used to cry at night.

G But it is strange, isn't it, that of all the sports a woman should choose to excel in, Rose chose the one that men measure their virility by?

Extension

Discuss these questions with two or three other students.

1 Why do you think the TV interviewers ask Rose about Italy and her boyfriend? Do you think they would ask the same sort of questions when talking to a male footballer?
2 Why do you think there are not so many women footballers as men? How does this compare with other sports?

Unit 13 Film reviews

Reading skills: Keeping your purpose in mind by thinking about the text type and content

Exam focus: Part 4 Multiple matching
  – preparing by predicting
  – reading to time

Theme: Film – see page 84 for a Part 4 practice test on the same theme

In this unit you are going to read some film reviews from a magazine.

Keeping your purpose in mind

Work with another student and answer the question.

Which of the following do you normally find in film reviews in newspapers and magazines? Put a tick in the correct column.

	Normally in a film review	Not normally in a film review
1 The reviewer's opinion of the film		
2 The plot or story		
3 A biography of the main actor		
4 A brief description of the main characters		
5 Technical information about the cameras		
6 The audience's opinion of the film		
7 Comparison with other films		
8 The type of film it is		

EXAM TIP 33

In Part 4 of the exam, it will help you to keep your purpose in mind while you are reading if you prepare by first thinking about the type of text you are going to read and the kind of content you expect it to cover.

Exam practice: Part 4 Multiple matching – preparing by predicting

1 Look at questions 1–15 below. Give yourself five minutes to check you
understand them.

Which film(s) could be described as the following film type?

science fiction | 1 | | 2 |

romance | 3 |

courtroom drama | 4 |

documentary | 5 |

biography | 6 | | 7 |

Which of the film plots could be summarised as follows?

It is about a nun who visited violent prisoners. | 8 |

Fate and fortune keep changing during the story. | 9 |

It is a fantasy about a possible terrible disease. | 10 |

It is an investigation with a strange result. | 11 |

About which of the films does the reviewer have the following opinion?

It presents a rather favourable picture. | 12 |

The director does a good job but it is rather a weak film. | 13 |

It is superficially brutal and cruel. | 14 |

It is almost perfect. | 15 |

2 Work with another student. Discuss what a science fiction, a romance, a courtroom
drama, a documentary and a biography might be about. Try to think of examples of each
type of film that you have seen.

3 Discuss these questions with your partner.

What is the difference between a summary of the plot and the reviewer's opinion?

Which of the following phrases refer to the plot of the film and which to the reviewer's
opinion? Write O or P in each box.

1 the film fails   ☐
2 Sam saves the world   ☐
3 little more than competent ☐
4 they all become victims ☐
5 it charts his life and career ☐
6 it is a bit over-sweet   ☐

59

Exam practice: Part 4 Multiple matching – reading to time

1 Give yourself two minutes only (two minutes is a long time!) to read about film A. Highlight or underline all the phrases which refer to the plot and all the phrases which refer to the reviewer's opinion. Then think what sort of film it is and put the letter A against the relevant questions on page 59.

2 Now continue reading and answering the questions, allowing two minutes for each film.

Films released on video this month

A   Ghosts from the Past

Director Rob Reiner has, in *Ghosts from the Past*, come up with little more than a competent TV movie. Alec Baldwin plays investigative lawyer Bobby DeLaughter, who re-opens the 30-year-old
5   case of murdered black political leader Medgar Evers. He puts white racist Byron De La Beckwith on trial for a third time, the previous two trials in 1963 having ended with the juries undecided.
10   There are references to the disappearing values of the old American South where whites ruled over blacks and to the progress made by the blacks over the previous three decades, but the film fails to develop any strong commentary.
15   Ultimately, Reiner's attention to detail is that of a documentary maker – a curious approach for one of Hollywood's most versatile and skilled storytellers.

B   Outbreak

Something's worrying scientist Sam Keogh
20   (Dustin Hoffman). It's a million times smaller than him and it is about to destroy the world – well a pretty town in California, anyway. Can Sam save the world from the killer virus? And can he also save his failing marriage? Only an actor
25   like Dustin Hoffman could succeed in this multi-million dollar nonsense which moves suddenly

from total absurdity – vast crowd scenes with everyone sneezing and coughing – to the totally terrifying with incredibly exciting helicopter stunts. If you enjoy a combination of political   30 conspiracy films and disaster movies, then *Outbreak* could be catching.

C   Dead Man Walking

Dead Man Walking is based on the true story of Sister Helen Prejean, a nun who wrote of two condemned murderers whom she visited regularly   35 in Death Row. Susan Sarandon plays her, while Sean Penn plays Matthew Poncelet – a sort of mixture of characters from Prejean's biography – whose friend she becomes in the face of enormous hostility from colleagues, victims' families and   40 even the murderer himself. Written and directed by Tim Robbins, *Dead Man Walking* is a moderate film, almost old-fashioned in its approach to human values. Though it moves slowly and carefully towards its conclusion,   45 without shocking twists or turns, it is dramatic in the truest sense of the word. A near faultless movie.

D   Jude

A humble stone worker from a country village wants to become a scholar. But he falls in love   50 with Sue, with whom he can share his deepest

feelings; unfortunately she is also his cousin and Jude goes through a pitiless series of sufferings. Every time something goes right for him and Sue,
55 something goes wrong within five minutes. This is a story of frustrated love and ambition.

Most importantly, Christopher Eccleston (Jude) and Kate Winslet (Sue) convince us they are in love to different, varying degrees. Strangely, this
60 is where most love stories don't work on screen. Winterbottom's direction is both solid and cool, classic and modern. A brilliantly made, very moving film.

E	Mandela

This documentary charts Mandela's life and
65 career from his childhood in a small African village through Johannesburg in the forties, his career as a lawyer, and his involvement with the African National Congress in the 1950s. It covers his years as a freedom fighter and as the world's
70 most famous political prisoner, to his final release and his election to the Presidency of the new republic of South Africa.

Mandela is a bit over-sweet, and at times seems like an advertisement for the new government. At other times it is more like a modern documentary. 75
There's also no sense that Mandela had to be without pity to win; he's too much of a nice old man.

F	The Relic

Set in a natural history museum and dealing very superficially with the question of evolution, *The*   80
Relic reminds you of the *Alien* series. After the terrible murder of one of the museum's security people, the museum staff bring in the police, headed by Lieutenant D'Agosta (played by Tom Sizemore). Together with top museum biologist   85
Margo Green (played by Penelope Ann Miller), D'Agosta comes to realise that the murderer is in fact a monster, related to a horrific creature of South American mythology. Security staff, scientists and police officers all become victims of 90
the creature's feeding craze.

Films like this only really work if they play on deep psychological fears that we all share. Otherwise what you have is just blood and violence, and that's what *The Relic* is.   95

EXAM TIP 35

In the exam you will have about twenty minutes for Part 4. You must organise your time. A good way to do so is to allow five minutes to study the reading purpose and ten to fifteen minutes to read the text and answer the questions. If there are six sections to the text, this means about two minutes for each section.

Extension

Still with your partner, discuss the following questions.

1 Which of the six films you have read about would you most like to see? Why?
2 Which film would you least like to see? Why?
3 The film *Jude* was originally a book. Which do you prefer, reading the novel or watching the film of the novel?
4 What about the novel of the film? Have you ever read one?
5 Which film have you seen most recently? Tell your partner about it.

Unit 14 Goodbye to film heroes

Reading skills:	Revising techniques for getting an overall picture
	Dealing with difficult words by looking for clues to meaning in the text
	Responding to the text by asking intelligent questions
Exam focus:	Part 3 Gapped text
Theme:	Film – see page 90 for a Part 3 practice test on the same theme

Getting an overall picture

1 Read the first paragraph of the text below and answer the questions.

   1 What did stuntmen and stuntwomen do?
   2 Why are stunt people quickly losing their jobs?

2 Look quickly through the whole text. Underline or highlight phrases containing the word *stunt*. Then work with another student and answer the questions.

   1 What do you think a *stunt co-ordinator* does?
   2 Can you think of an example of an *extravagant stunt*?
   3 What is another way of saying *stunt people are becoming extinct*?
   4 What are *genuine stunts*?
   5 What do you think a *cartoon stunt* is?

EXAM TIP 36

You learned the technique of getting an overall picture by looking for words which occur again and again in a text in Unit 1. You can often get a better overall picture by studying the phrases in which the repeated words appear. This, combined with reading the first paragraph, will help you when you come to read intensively.

Death of the stuntmen

Hollywood's true heroes have become redundant. Stuntmen and stuntwomen who entertained cinemagoers by falling from the sky, swimming with sharks and rolling fast
5 cars have been replaced by technology. After surviving generations of screen fights, high falls and setting fire to themselves, the people behind the top actors' most exciting scenes have had nearly all their work substituted by computer-generated stunts. 10

Advances in special effects mean that the most dangerous and costly stunts can be achieved by mixing computer graphics with live action. **1** ☐

15 The end of the stuntman was signalled by blockbusters such as *Volcano*, starring Tommy Lee Jones, *Titanic* with Kate Winslet and *The Lost World*, Steven Spielberg's sequel to *Jurassic Park*. **2** ☐

20 Wayne Michaels, one of Britain's top stunt co-ordinators and the man who did a 250-metre bungee jump in the James Bond movie *Goldeneye*, said that at first studios tended to use computers for more extrava-

25 gant stunts.

'But they went on to do far more common and mundane things with computers, such as falling down stairs,' he said. 'As a result, stunt people are becoming extinct. **3** ☐ '

30 In the mid-1990s there were 12,000 registered stunt people, but more than half of them had difficulty finding work. Loren Janes, a co-founder of the Stuntmen's Association of Motion Pictures and Television,

35 said that, by 1997, teams of stuntmen and stuntwomen had found their work curtailed by technology. 'Six or seven teams would be working on a film. Then, after a few days, the producers would come in and say, "You

40 can go home. **4** ☐ "'

The reason was simple: cost. Computer technology pioneered in movies such as *Terminator 2* fell in price and became capable of creating stunts which would either be

45 too expensive or too dangerous to attempt. One example was in *Mission Impossible*, starring Tom Cruise. In a scene where Cruise flies for 35 metres through the air from an exploding helicopter on to the back

50 of a speeding train in the Channel tunnel, the image of the actor was simply superimposed on the scene using computers.

5 ☐ A fall from 50 metres into water or an air bag can now be achieved for a tenth of the cost. 55

With the rise of digital technology, insurance companies became more reluctant to cover genuine stunts. 'If they know it can be done safely with visual effects, the companies will not insure real stunts,' said Simon 60 Crane, a veteran stunt co-ordinator.

Many in the industry believe stunt people should develop expertise in the new technology, acting as advisers on the virtual stunts. **6** ☐ Some, however, think that 65 stuntmen can survive in their traditional careers. Peter Brayham, a British stunt veteran who drove a car through a plate-glass window at the beginning of *The Professionals* television series, said: 70 'We call successful stunts "setting the audience alight". **7** ☐ The audience won't accept cartoon stunts for too long.'

Dealing with difficult words

Find the word *blockbusters* in the text (line 16).

Read the sentence containing the word *blockbusters* and look for ways to help you understand the word.

Blockbusters is followed by *such as* which means the same as *for example*. So *Volcano, starring Tommy Lee Jones* and *Titanic with Kate Winslet* are *blockbusters*. So a *blockbuster* must be a sort of film.

Now do the same with these words. Look at each sentence and try to find clues which will help you with their meanings.

1 sequel (line 19)
2 mundane (line 27)
3 curtailed (line 36)
4 plate-glass (line 69)

EXAM TIP 37

You can often ignore some words in a text and still understand the meaning. You can sometimes guess the approximate meaning of other words by gathering information about them. This will mean reading the whole text first, before trying to work out the meanings.

Responding to the text

Work with another student. Read through the whole text slowly. Stop when you come to each numbered space and try to answer the question with the same number below.

1 What is the result of mixing computer graphics with live action?
2 Why have these films in particular been mentioned?
3 What do you think stunt people feel about that?
4 Can you guess why they said it?
5 Can you think of any other examples of stunts which would be too expensive or dangerous to attempt with real stuntmen?
6 What is the alternative?
7 Does Peter Brayham think that computers are capable of 'setting the audience alight'?

EXAM TIP 38

Sometimes an interactive technique such as asking questions as you read can help you with the gapped text task in Part 3 of the exam. If you ask intelligent questions at the numbered gaps, you may find that the lettered sentences or paragraphs are intelligent answers.

Exam practice: Part 3 Gapped text

Choose from the sentences A–H below the one which fits each gap (1–7) in the text. There is one extra sentence which you do not need to use. Use your answers to the questions on page 64 to help you.

A Each is packed with computerised stunts.

B Similarly, when Pierce Brosnan appeared in *Dante's Peak* running in front of a fireball, the burning mass was, in fact, computer-generated and added at a later stage of production.

C This enables the actors themselves to appear as if they are performing the stunts.

D We've worked out how to do it on computer.

E The dangers are too great and directors are no longer willing to take the risk.

F Computers don't do that.

G It's not a popular view but it is a fact of life.

H Otherwise, they will be left with little else to do than perform in the occasional fist fight.

Extension

Work with another student. Discuss these questions.

1 Think of some of your favourite stunt scenes in the films you have seen. Try to describe them.
2 When you watch action films, can you tell the difference between a genuine stunt and a computer-generated stunt?
3 What work possibilities are there now for adventurous people who enjoy taking risks?
4 How many other jobs can you think of where computers have taken away the need for people?

Unit 15 How to be a movie star

Getting an overall picture

1 Look quickly at the text on the opposite page. Read the introduction, in italics.

2 Work with another student. Discuss these questions.

1 In good cinema acting, is there normally more speech than gesture or less?
2 Should screen actors express feelings firstly through gestures, or should they deliver their lines first, then use gestures? Perhaps the lines and the gestures should come at the same time?
3 Do you think that screen gestures are natural? Should screen actors try to copy exactly what they see in real life? Should they exaggerate? Or should they underplay their gestures?

EXAM TIP 39

In Part 1 of the exam there is often an introduction to the text which you do not have to choose a heading or a summary sentence for. Read introductions like these very carefully: they can help you to get an overall picture before reading the whole text.

Responding to the text

1 Read the text carefully. Highlight or underline phrases which show that the writer agrees or disagrees with the opinions you gave in the last activity.

2 Work with the same partner. Compare the phrases you have highlighted or underlined. Discuss how far you agree with the writer and with each other.

EXAM TIP 40

A good way to respond to non-fiction texts is by comparing your opinions to those of the writer.

SECRETS OF SCREEN ACTING

Gesture and speech – how much of each and which should come first?
How natural should they be? Screen acting is very different from real life.

In real life, when a group of people are talking, their eyes tend to go towards the person who is talking at the moment. In the cinema, when there are two actors on the screen, one talking and the other listening, I believe that the audience watches the listener more than the speaker. This is quite logical since we can tell from the sound of the voice more or less what
5 is on the face of the speaker – what we do not know is what the listener is thinking or feeling, and so we watch her.

Try this exercise. Ask an actor to sit on a chair and act for about thirty seconds. Record the results. Nearly everyone who does the exercise speaks for the full thirty seconds. They could have scratched their heads, started and stopped or given lots of reactions and few words.
10 They could, in fact, have presented what they have watched thousands of times on the screen; but no, what usually happens is that they present word-heavy performances that represent nothing they have either seen on screen or experienced in real life.

In real life, our faces tend to reflect what we have just said. On screen, a picture of one character speaking will be followed shortly by a picture of another character. The viewers
15 do not want to know how the first person feels about something she has just said, they want to know what the other person feels about it. So if the actor wants to convey extra information with a facial expression, the best time to do this is before the speech.

Choose a simple reaction, like swallowing. Ask someone to do this a few times. Film the results, and then speak some dialogue just before each swallow so you see the pictures you
20 have filmed while you hear yourself saying such things as:
'I think you're very nice'   (swallow)
'You've just won the lottery!'   (swallow)
You will be very impressed with what wonderful, truthful and subtle performances you have put on the screen even though you know the person swallowing was not feeling a
25 thing – except perhaps a little foolish.

I was once talking with a group of actors about positive listening. One actor was upset, claiming that she hated watching actors pull faces and that listening should be what we would do in real life. I immediately got her with another actor and told her not to listen to what he was saying, but to spend her energies in giving a whole range of expressions. When
30 I asked her 'How was that?' she replied 'Terrible', but we all – the other actors and I in chorus – went 'It was wonderful!'. Which it was.

| 6 | |

Let's talk about props. Take a pencil. Now, it is not going to change a lot in the next few minutes, but if you pick it up, it becomes a way of allowing the audience into your thoughts and feelings. If you pick it up delicately or grab it, this would show two different emotions
35 and attitudes. If you throw it on the table or break it in half, you have given more messages.

| 7 | |

In order to achieve good results with gestures, you have to get good at them – and that means research and practice. Research means watching yourself in real-life situations and finding out what is your vocabulary of moves and gestures. Watch other people in the underground, in shops, at parties: what do they do that can be added to your vocabulary? Then watch
40 screens, see what other actors do, see which bits you can steal – I mean adapt – for your own use.

Analysing the text

1 Find the following phrases in the text.

   1 *what* usually happens is that they present word-heavy performances (line 11)
   2 In real life, our faces tend to reflect *what* we have just said (line 13)
   3 You will be very impressed with *what* wonderful, truthful and subtle performances you have put on the screen (lines 23–24)
   4 finding out *what is* your vocabulary of moves and gestures (lines 37–38)

For each phrase, try to replace the word(s) in italics with an alternative from the list below.

   the
   the things
   the thing that
   (nothing – just take it away and the sentence doesn't change its meaning)

2 Now find these phrases in the text.

   1 we can tell from the sound of the voice more or less *what is* on the face of the speaker (lines 4–5)
   2 *what* we do not know is *what the listener is thinking or feeling* (line 5)
   3 They could, in fact, have presented *what they have watched thousands of times on the screen* (lines 10–11)
   4 listening should be *what we would do in real life* (lines 27–28)

Replace the words in italics with one of the expressions below.

   the thing that
   our normal activity
   the expression
   a very commonly observed scene
   the other person's thoughts and emotions

EXAM TIP 41

Be careful when you come to phrases beginning with *what*. It can introduce several different types of phrase. It is a good idea to try to put these phrases into your own words to help you understand them.

Exam practice: Part 1 Multiple matching

Choose the most suitable summary sentence from the list A–H for each part (1–7) of the text on page 67. There is one extra sentence which you do not need to use.

A Acting is more about watching others than doing things yourself.

B The timing of facial gestures and words depends on the 'rhythm' of film.

C Most people equate acting with speaking despite their real-life and cinema experiences.

D Observation and practice are the keys to success.

E Simple mechanical gestures can seem very meaningful on screen.

F Facial gestures on screen do not have to be life-like: the more expressive they are, the better they work.

G Objects can be used to express a wide range of feelings.

H Our attention has different targets in real life and in the cinema.

Extension

Work with another student. Discuss these questions.

1 Would you like to be a screen actor? Why? Why not?
2 Who are your favourite screen actors? Why?
3 Think of a scene in a film you have seen where the actors do not speak. Describe the scene and say how you knew what they were thinking and feeling.
4 How does screen acting differ from real life? Look back over all the sections of the text to help you discuss.

Review unit

Review of techniques for:
– getting an overall picture
– responding to the text
– analysing the text
– keeping your purpose in mind and ignoring irrelevant information
– dealing with difficult words

Getting an overall picture

Remember:

* In Parts 1–3 of the exam, in order to understand efficiently and effectively, you need an overall picture before you start reading carefully.
* You must build up an overall picture as quickly as possible.
* There are different techniques for getting an overall picture, according to the type of text.

Work with another student. Put the letters in the underlined words in these sentences in the correct order and find eight techniques for getting an overall picture.

1 Look for <u>qtnfereu</u> words, words which occur again and again.
2 Use any visual material such as <u>cuptirse</u> or <u>gmidasra</u>.
3 Use the <u>eiltt</u> at the beginning of the text, if there is one.
4 Use the <u>troiduntinco</u>, if there is one.
5 Read the first <u>ghaapprra</u> or the first few <u>enlsi</u>.
6 Look for names of people, towns and countries with <u>platcai</u> letters.
7 Think about your own <u>gndkeelwo</u> of the subject or topic.
8 Prepare yourself for the <u>leyts</u> of the piece.

Still working with your partner, discuss which text type each technique is most suitable for. Complete the chart.

Text type	Technique
stories	
biographies	
newspaper and magazine articles	
non-fiction books	

What other techniques for getting an overall picture do you know? And when you have got an overall picture, what is the next thing you should do before starting to read carefully?

Responding to the text

Remember:

* In Parts 1–3 of the exam, in order to understand a text properly, you have to respond to it as you are reading.
* This often means stopping during reading.
* But you must not stop at difficult words. Stop at the end of each section of the text.

1 There are many different ways in which you can respond to a text. These key words might help you to remember some of them.

> hear   relate   form   rephrase   summarise   visualise   ask

Divide into two teams. Try to remember the techniques for responding to a text using the key words in the list. The winner is the first team to complete notes similar to those given in the example. Look back at the exam tips to help you.

hear (Exam Tip 3)
respond to the text by trying to 'hear' dialogue ....

relate (Exam Tip 8)
....

form (Exam Tip 18)
....

rephrase (Exam Tip 23)
....

summarise (Exam Tip 26)
....

visualise (Exam Tip 28)
....

ask (Exam Tip 38)
....

2 Work with another student. Try to think up an acronym to help you remember all the techniques. (If you take the tips in the above order, you get the acronym 'HRFRSVA', which is not easy to remember! Look back at Exam Tips 12, 31 and 40 for some other key words to make it easier.)

Analysing the text

Remember:

* To answer some multiple choice comprehension questions in Part 2 of the exam and to complete the gapped text in Part 3, you may have to analyse parts of the text in detail.

1 Work with another student. Read this short text and follow the instructions below it.

> Having found the first exercise too difficult, I left it and went straight on to the second one. If I was going to finish on time, I would have to work as quickly as possible. What I hadn't realised was how long the test would be.

1 Underline the participle and put a circle round the subject of the first sentence. Rewrite the sentence to clarify the meaning. (Look again at Exam Tip 21 in Unit 8.)
2 What do *it* and *one* refer to? (Look again at Exam Tip 9 in Unit 3 and 13 in Unit 5.)
3 Which connecting word could you put before *If* at the beginning of the second sentence? (Look again at Exam Tip 19 in Unit 7.)
4 Does *If I was going to finish on time* refer to an impossible situation or an intention? (Look again at Exam Tip 24 in Unit 9.)
5 Find an alternative word or phrase for *What*. (Look again at Exam Tip 41 in Unit 15.)

2 Still with the same partner, discuss the pictures below. What techniques for analysing text do they illustrate?

Look back at Exam Tip 29 in Unit 11 and 32 in Unit 12 to check your answers.

1

2

Keeping your purpose in mind and ignoring irrelevant information

Read the following text as quickly as you can. Find six pieces of advice to help you with Part 4 of the exam.

Part 4 of Paper 1 of the Cambridge First Certificate in English (FCE) examination has a different orientation from the other parts. While in Parts 1, 2 and 3 you really have to get down to the meaning of what the writer is saying, in Part 4 you have to get information from the text and nothing more. You are given a brief description of the text type at the beginning of Part 4 and it is a good idea to start by thinking about what the text might contain.

You are also told the information you have to collect from the text before you start reading. It is a good idea to study this carefully too. This briefing doesn't usually contain words or expressions from the text itself, but it does use words and expressions which are similar to those you will find in it. Identifying the key words in this pre-reading briefing will help you keep your purpose in mind and ignore irrelevant information when you actually start reading.

When you find words or expressions in the text which have a similar meaning to the key words you have identified it's a good idea to underline them so that, when you've finished reading, you can easily check back against the briefing and make sure you have the right information.

This is not the only thing you can do. You might also like to try, when going through the briefing, predicting words or phrases which are likely to turn up in the text itself. After all, when you read informative material, a lot of your understanding is prepared for by the predictions you make, so it seems logical to make a conscious effort to predict.

Finally, and most importantly, you must use your time wisely. Decide on the best way of dividing up the fifteen to twenty minutes you have. In the exam, put a watch or small clock in front of you and keep looking at it so that you can keep strict control over your time.

If you bear these strategies in mind, you should be able to get through Part 4 without difficulty. As with the other parts of the examination, success has a lot to do with your own confidence in yourself: if you feel confident, you are sure to do a better job than if you do not. This book has had the main aim of increasing your confidence by offering practical strategies and techniques. Of course, you may not want to use all of them, but by using some, at least, you should be able to face the examination positively and confidently. Good luck!

Look back at Exam Tips 5 and 6 in Unit 2, 16 in Unit 6, and 33, 34 and 35 in Unit 13 to remind yourself of the relevant advice.

Dealing with difficult words

Remember:

* Almost any text you read will have some words in it that you have never seen before.
* In Parts 1–3 of the exam, read the whole text before going back to deal with new words.
* Decide whether or not the new words are important to your understanding of the text.
* Don't panic!

1 Work with another student. Use the questionnaire below to find out what type of reader you are when it comes to dealing with difficult words.

Questionnaire

1 In order to keep your confidence while you are reading under exam conditions do you

   a) underline everything you understand?
   b) underline all the words you don't understand?
   c) underline nothing?
   d) underline everything whether you understand it or not?

2 When you find an unfamiliar word in a text, do you

   a) see if you can break it down into parts?
   b) underline it and come back to it at some stage?
   c) ignore it completely?
   d) look at it for a very long time and hope you will understand?

3 When you start reading a new text, do you

   a) use an 'overall picture' technique and then think about what it will probably contain?
   b) read word for word and stop when you come to an unfamiliar word?
   c) start reading immediately, stopping to think when you have made sense of the first few sentences?
   d) read through the text without stopping, even if it gets very difficult to understand?

4 You find this sentence in a piece of fiction writing:

Lord Darley came along the road riding his young cob.

   a) You decide on the meaning of *cob* by looking at the context, in particular, the words *riding* and *young*.
   b) You underline *cob* and copy the word into a note book under the letter C.
   c) You ignore the word *cob*: it's probably not important how Lord Darley came along the road.
   d) You try to take the word *cob* apart to see if you can understand it from its root.

2 Analyse your questionnaire results like this.

If you chose mostly a) answers:
You are quite a methodical reader. You read carefully and make use of some techniques to help you.

If you chose mostly b) answers:
You are a studious reader. You read in order to improve your general knowledge of English. But remember that the FCE exam tests your reading ability, not your ability to use a text as a study tool.

If you chose mostly c) answers:
You are a very confident reader indeed. Be careful! Your confidence may make you overlook details in the text at times.

Of course you didn't choose mostly d) answers!

Practice tests

How to use the practice tests

The five practice tests which follow are very similar to Paper 1 of the First Certificate in English (FCE) exam. Use them to test your progress and help you practise your reading skills for the exam.

You can do the tests in any order and you can do the individual parts of a test in any order. You do not have to do all four parts of each practice test at the same time.

All the test material reflects one of the five unit themes and you may like to do some test practice in conjunction with individual units.

Key to themes		
Education	Practice test 2	Part 4
	Practice test 3	Part 3
	Practice test 4	Part 2
	Practice test 5	Part 1
Holidays	Practice test 1	Part 1
	Practice test 3	Part 4
	Practice test 4	Part 3
	Practice test 5	Part 2
Animals	Practice test 1	Part 2
	Practice test 2	Part 1
	Practice test 4	Part 4
	Practice test 5	Part 3
Success	Practice test 1	Part 3
	Practice test 2	Part 2
	Practice test 3	Part 1
	Practice test 5	Part 4
Film	Practice test 1	Part 4
	Practice test 2	Part 3
	Practice test 3	Part 2
	Practice test 4	Part 1

However you use these practice tests, try to do at least one test under exam conditions. Give yourself 75 minutes to complete the entire paper.

Remember your reading skills!

By the time you have completed Units 1–15, you will know a great many skills and strategies to help you with your reading. When you are doing the practice tests and in the exam itself, don't forget to use them.

For Parts 1–3 of the exam, try to get an overall picture before you start, then use the techniques you have learned for dealing with difficult words and your text analysis skills to help you understand the text. Responding to the text will often help your understanding too.

In Part 4, try to keep your purpose in mind and ignore irrelevant information.

A good way of revising the techniques you have learned is to read through all the exam tips in Units 1–15. The summary chart below will help you find the relevant units to refer back to.

Reading skills and strategies – where to find what		Unit
Getting an overall picture	from words which occur again and again	1, 5, 14
	from the title and illustration	3, 4, 5
	from the first few lines	7, 14
	by reading the first and last paragraphs and thinking about the text type and style	8
	by using a combination of techniques	9
	from the title and subtitle	10
	by using your own knowledge of a subject	11
	from capitalised words	12
	from the introduction	15
Dealing with difficult words	by concentrating on the words you do understand	1
	by breaking them down into parts	4
	by using the context	5
	by using a combination of techniques	6
	by looking for clues to meaning in the text	14
Responding to the text	by trying to 'hear' dialogue	1
	by relating it to personal experience	3
	by 'having a conversation' with the writer	4
	by forming an opinion about the characters	7
	by paraphrasing while you read	9
	by summarising what it says	10
	by trying to visualise what it describes	11
	by analysing the writer's intentions	12
	by asking intelligent questions	14
	by comparing your opinions with those of the writer	15
Analysing the text	reference words	3, 5, 12
	logical connections	7, 11
	participles	8
	linking words	9
	verb tenses	12
	phrases beginning with *what*	15
Keeping your purpose in mind	by using one- or two-word summaries	2, 6
	by thinking about the text type and content	13
Ignoring irrelevant information	by highlighting or underlining relevant information	2, 6

Practice test 1

Part 1

You are going to read an article about careers in tourism. Choose the most suitable heading from the list **A–H** for each part (**1–6**) of the article. There is one extra heading which you do not need to use. There is an example at the beginning (**0**).

A	Surprise yourself
B	Changing patterns
C	How to get started
D	Meeting the challenge
E	Rewards for the right person
F	Spoilt for choice
G	A new approach
H	A growth industry

Why choose tourism?

0   **H**

Tourism is one of the world's biggest and fastest growing industries. Increased leisure time, higher standards of living and better transport are just some of the reasons why the tourism industry is expanding in the UK and overseas. Interesting and exciting career opportunities are opening up as the industry continues to grow.

1

Jobs in tourism have often been regarded as 'seasonal' and 'low paid' but things are changing fast. Summer is not the only time we like to take our holidays. Short breaks in spring, autumn and winter coupled with the vital business tourism market mean that operators are now busy throughout the year and therefore require staff on a permanent basis.

2

Working in tourism is not for everybody. This is a 'people' business where customer care and high standards of service are essential. Some occupations may also require you to work long and often unsociable hours. The big plus factor is the pleasure of knowing you have helped people to enjoy their holidays or ensured that a conference has run smoothly.

3

The industry consists of a huge variety of organisations, including both the public and the private sector, and the career options are therefore many and varied. You could choose to work as a Tourism Officer in the UK, responsible for marketing and visitor services, or you might opt for the role of Tour Guide, travelling around the country with groups of holidaymakers from all over the world. The airline business could be of interest to you or you might like to try Event Management, which could involve helping to arrange anything from a local festival to a major international event such as the Tall Ships.

4

Whatever your interest you will need to have both the enthusiasm and the qualifications. More colleges and universities are now offering courses to equip you with the skills needed for a successful career in tourism. Many also provide the chance for work experience, giving you the opportunity to discover at first hand what the job may involve. It could also provide you with some vital contacts for your future career.

5

Newton Rigg College in Cumbria, not far from the Lake District, is now offering a Higher National Diploma in Sustainable Tourism. The two-year course involves studying the tourism industry and the use of the countryside and includes a six-week work placement opportunity. As Newton Rigg is also an associate college of the University of Central Lancashire, there are opportunities for students to progress from this course to degree level. An increasing awareness of conservation and the greater emphasis now being placed on tourism projects and developments which are truly 'sustainable' mean that employers will be seeking skills and qualifications in these areas. The course is already attracting applicants from this country and from as far afield as Hong Kong.

6

Why not consider the possibilities of a career in tourism? There are opportunities for all kinds of people, from young school leavers to university graduates, and there are many chances for 'sideways' moves into any one of a large number of related areas. So if you think that working in tourism means just selling package holidays or a couple of months' work in a hotel, you may be pleasantly surprised.

Part 2

You are going to read an extract from a novel about a dog-detective. For questions **7–14**, choose the answer (**A**, **B**, **C** or **D**) which you think fits best according to the text.

'Track!' said my master.

Like any obedient tracker-dog who has received the command he most loves, I gave a bark of excitement, put my nose down to the pavement and sniffed. The pavement was rich with smells. Even in the high-class residential area where we
5 were working, the stones held traces of subtle and complex fragrances. As I searched for the scent that would give me a clue to the trail of the guilty man, my tail wagged slowly, thoughtfully, delightedly. Work was like play to me; I enjoyed it.

A small group of people gathered behind us. Among these onlookers was the
10 old caretaker of the building next door to ours. He spoke in a scornful voice: 'You actually think your dog might catch a thief three days after the event?' My master said nothing, but I'm sure he must have smiled. I did not turn to look. I knew he would not speak unless it was to give me a new command.

I needed to concentrate. My task was difficult. I had to pick out one scent
15 among the many that lay about and then track it to its source.

'You're wasting your time,' said the caretaker. I looked at him without raising my head. He was running his hand over his fat stomach. His rough palm and smooth shirt combined to make a slight noise. It was part of my training to be aware – often it is only a little whisper of a noise that alerts you to the drawing of
20 a weapon. But of course the ageing caretaker was going to do no such thing. There was no smell of fear or nervousness about him. He was merely being clever and talkative. He handled his stomach as though it was a badge of authority.

'I've seen many tracker-dogs in my time,' said the caretaker to the onlookers. 'I served with the police years ago. We would never have thought of using a
25 tracker-dog to find a car thief. Impossible. Everyone knows that dogs are useless in such matters. He's got his car back, so what's the use of parking it again in the same place and trying to pick up one scent among the hundreds on this pavement? It's like asking the dog to do a crossword puzzle!'

In a sense he was right. I'm sure there's no need to tell you that, just as a dog's
30 hearing is much better than a human being's, so his sense of smell distinguishes one thing from another far better than the most powerful magnifying glass in the world. If Sherlock Holmes could work out that a man had had an egg for breakfast by seeing the yellow stain on his mouth, a trained dog could tell you whether the hen that laid the egg was healthy or not.

35 I know it sounds funny and I mean it to be. But I'm not exaggerating. A dog can tell you – provided you understand a dog's way of communicating – all this and more without even setting eyes on the man he is investigating.

But here the ground was criss-crossed in a complex knot of different smells and scents and tracks. To untie it and follow one of them, seemed like asking for
40 a miracle.

7 How did the dog-narrator react to the command to track?

    A It did what was asked because it was obedient.

    B It was happy, even though it wasn't trained for the task.

    C It was frustrated because there were so many smells.

    D It was excited because it enjoyed tracking.

8 What do we learn about the place where the story was set?

    A It was a complicated area and rather smelly.

    B It was full of rich people's houses.

    C The buildings were made of stone.

    D The pavements were in very good condition.

9 What does *many* in line 15 refer to?

    A new commands

    B difficult tasks

    C scents on the ground

    D onlookers

10 What did the dog-narrator notice about the caretaker?

    A By the sound he made he might have been pulling out a gun.

    B His clothes were of varying quality.

    C He spoke in a whispering tone.

    D By his gestures it seemed that he was not feeling very well.

11 Why was the dog-narrator sure that the caretaker was not dangerous?

    A It thought he was too intelligent to use violence.

    B It had seen he was wearing a badge to show he was a kind of policeman.

    C It did not sense that he was afraid.

    D It realised that he was too old to be dangerous.

12 What did the caretaker think about using a dog to catch a car thief?

    A He was hopeful and encouraging towards the dog's owner.

    B He was sure it would not work.

    C He wished the police had come up with the idea.

    D He thought it was just a game for the dog.

13 What does the dog-narrator tell us about its sense of smell?

    A It is not as good as its sense of hearing.

    B It can achieve what a human's sight can and much more.

    C It can only give us more details about what a human has already discovered.

    D When there are many scents together, it cannot distinguish one from another.

14 According to the passage, a dog can

    A give you a lot of information if you can communicate with it.

    B tell you many things without seeing you.

    C provide you with a way of communicating with it.

    D do more than just investigate people it can't see.

Part 3

You are going to read an article about someone who gave up a successful life. Eight sentences have been removed from the article. Choose from the sentences **A–I** the one which fits each gap (**15–21**). There is one extra sentence which you do not need to use. There is an example at the beginning (**0**).

How to get out

Peter Mantle used to live in a two-bedroom flat in London with a tiny terrace. If he had a moment in his 15-hour working day to look up from his computer at the view from the window, he saw a grey block of flats. **0** **I** Then he went on holiday to Ireland. Ten years later, he now runs a salmon fishery and lives in a 15-bedroom house. The view from his windows has been described as one of the most beautiful valleys in Europe.

15 When an estate agent told him that the place was for sale, Peter knew it was a once-in-a-lifetime opportunity. 'I made the decision overnight,' he admits. 'My girl-friend thought I had gone crazy and my father was so angry he wouldn't speak to me for a week.'

Peter hadn't planned to abandon his career, but the fishery simply took his breath away. 'Through the most spectacular scenery, we saw this old house and I thought, wow!' **16**

'And the timing was right, job-wise,' he says. 'I loved what I was doing, but I regularly worked 100 hours a week. It was very stimulating and exciting but very unhealthy.' Shortly before his Irish holiday, Peter had collapsed on a business flight between Milan and Rome. **17** 'Doctors checked me out and said "There's nothing wrong with you except you smoke too much, you drink too much and you work far too hard".'

'So when I fell in love with the fishery, everything happened quickly. If it had been thought out, we probably would not have done it, because it was short-sighted and, in many ways, pretty stupid! Having quit, I had got no income and, apart from a little work as a financial journalist, I had no money at all. **18** It was a huge risk. I knew it could ruin us financially, and as a couple, because neither of us knew if we would adapt or even like it,' he admits. 'So we said we'd give it a trial year.'

An Irish bank agreed to a £250,000 loan so work could start restoring the fishery and, in the meantime, Peter rented a cottage. 'We allowed ourselves £100 a week, which covered living expenses and insurance – I still don't have a pension,' explains Peter. 'But in spite of this drop in earnings, we didn't suffer much. **19** But in Ireland, there weren't the same opportunities to spend, so even though we weren't earning very much, it didn't really hurt.'

20 'We're never going to get rich, but that's not what we really want. We just don't want to worry.' Peter advises anyone thinking of 'getting out' to beware of rose-coloured glasses. 'It's no good thinking everything's going to be very easy. It's not. **21** People tend to forget that.' That said, Peter has no regrets: 'Some of our friends come and see us, but they wouldn't swap places. Right now, there's nobody I'd swap places with either.'

A In London we might eat out three or four times a week, go to the cinema, as well as having to pay heavily for our house.

B I had no experience of running any kind of enterprise and no background in agriculture or fisheries.

C Within two months, he'd quit his job, sold his company shares and bought the house and its land for just over £200,000.

D 'I couldn't move my arms and legs and I was paralysed for about 20 minutes,' he recalls.

E So far Peter has spent over £1 million on his passion, but he's yet to make a profit.

F It was during the holiday that he had come across the fishery, then disused, and had fallen in love with it.

G Peter took possession of the fishery with some help from his family.

H You're just swapping the old life for a different set of pressures – pressures associated with having to survive sufficiently to finance what you want to do.

I He loved the excitement of his £60,000 job as director of a financial publishing company and the buzz of city life.

Part 4

You are going to read a guide to film locations – the places where some famous films were made. For questions **22–35**, choose from the films (**A–F**). Some of the films may be chosen more than once. There is an example at the beginning (**0**).

Of which film production do we find out the following?

One of the locations was used to represent two different places.	**0**	F
The location has a historical connection with the subject of the film.	**22**	
One of the locations was once recognised by someone watching the film.	**23**	
What you see in the film as one location is actually three different locations.	**24**	
One of the locations was, soon after, used for another film.	**25**	
The location was an old house which was, surprisingly, still more or less in its original condition.	**26**	
The choice of some of the locations was quite controversial.	**27**	
The director changed his filming plan to make full use of the location.	**28**	
A great house became a sort of theatre in the film.	**29**	
The obvious location had been modernised and so was not used.	**30**	

The location had been abandoned by its owners because of financial problems.	**31**	
The location was a combination of buildings from different historical periods.	**32**	
The location was successful because there were no cars, lorries or buses to get in the way.	**33**	
One of the locations has become a very popular place for people to go and stay.	**34**	
One of the locations was specially constructed with the weather in mind.	**35**	

On location – a film fan's guide to Britain and Ireland

Not all films are made in the studio. These days most films use real places, either as themselves or as somewhere completely different. Everyone must at some time have wondered where a film was actually made but until now there has never been a guide to film locations. So here goes!

A Black Beauty

The activity and business of nineteenth-century street life was recreated in the courtyard of one of England's great stately homes, Blenheim Palace, near Oxford. It was here that Winston Churchill was born and that Black Beauty worked pulling a taxi for Jerry Baker (played by David Thewlis), with the palace appearing in the background as an opera house. 'It was great,' says writer-director Caroline Thompson. 'It worked well for us because it was completely controllable – we didn't have to worry about traffic.'

B Four Weddings and a Funeral

With crowds of people going to see it again and again, many viewers must have wondered exactly where the four weddings and one funeral took place. One screening was interrupted by a shout of recognition when St. Michael's Church in Betchworth, Surrey, appeared on the screen. 'That's the church where I got married,' was the proud declaration. Bookings have increased tremendously for the honeymoon suite at the Crown Hotel in Amersham where Carrie (played by Andie McDowell) and Charles (played by Hugh Grant) get together after the first wedding.

C The Madness of King George

Thame Park, near Oxford, was the very interesting setting for this film. It was the home of Sophia Wykeham who was for a short time engaged to one of King George III's sons, the Duke of Clarence.

Alan Bennett, who wrote the film's script, based on his play *The Madness of King George III*, says: 'I'd no idea myself about the settings or the locations. I wrote the scenes and then they put them in the various settings. Thame Park is this kind of wonderful mixture of houses – eighteenth century and Tudor and medieval – and it had been bought by a Japanese consortium to turn into a hotel. They had more or less ruined it really. Then they went bankrupt and it was just left to fall down, so we took it over to do some scenes.'

D The Secret Garden

The Secret Garden became the 'Secret Gardens', plural, in the film of Frances Hodgson Burnett's popular children's book. Burnett had lived at Great Maytham Hall, in Kent, in the 1890s and it is thought that she based her overgrown secret garden on a neglected, high-walled garden there. The building has now been converted into flats. Finding the right garden turned out to be quite a problem for the film-makers, and they ended up with a combination of gardens from the north and south of England, and at Pinewood Studios. They shot at Allerton Park, in Yorkshire, and at Luton Hoo, near Luton. A third garden was laid out in the studios where, if rain prevented filming, everyone could retire indoors and shoot indoor scenes.

E Jane Eyre

Charlotte Brontë's story of Jane Eyre and Edward Rochester is brought to life at Haddon Hall, near Matlock in Derbyshire. The director, Franco Zeffirelli, had seen old prints of Haddon Hall, the imposing manor house of the Duke of Rutland, but was astonished to find how well preserved it was. 'It's a magnificent place – extraordinary,' he says. 'It's miraculous how this house has been kept for centuries intact. They haven't done any alterations.' Zeffirelli considered the terraced garden magnificent. He was at Haddon Hall for three weeks and changed his shooting script to maximise the use of the location.

F Braveheart

Filming began in June 1994 in Scotland, in Glen Nevis, beneath Britain's highest mountain and close to one of the principal locations for *Rob Roy* which arrived just a few weeks later. There was a lot of discussion when it was announced, just before production, that most of the shooting would be done in Ireland. Dunsoghly Castle, a modest fifteenth-century tower just outside Dublin, stood in for Edinburgh Castle, possibly the most famous ancient fortress in the British Isles, but it was thought that international audiences would never know the difference. The use the film-makers made of Trim Castle was even more daring. The castle, about 25 miles north west of Dublin, was used to represent both York and London. 'We just used two sides of the castle,' says production manager Mary Alleguen. 'We did York one side and London the other side.'

Practice test 2

Part 1

You are going to read an article about someone who can talk to animals. Choose the most suitable summary sentence from the list **A–I** for each part (**1–7**) of the article. There is one extra summary sentence which you do not need to use. There is an example at the beginning (**0**).

A There are two main working methods.

B Another animal professional accepts the truth.

C Getting permission to go ahead is important.

D Selective use of psychic power is vital.

E Solutions to problems are not just medical – or just for animals.

F An animal explains and its owner confirms.

G Problems need examining from different angles.

H An apparent contradiction is explained.

I Sometimes just one look is enough.

A day in the life of a pet psychic

0   I

I started communicating with animals while on holiday in Greece nearly thirty years ago; now I run a surgery from my home in London. Communicating with animals takes place on many different levels. You communicate with your eyes, your hands, with silence. Once, a nice couple came into the surgery with a very small dog. The way he was lying against his mistress, looking round him with an amazing expression on his face, he just made me laugh out loud. He felt like a complete clown. 'Is he a bit of a clown?' I asked. 'Absolutely,' they said. 'That's why his name is Coco.'

1

My first appointment is at 10 a.m. I always ask the animal if it's okay to communicate, because it can be very intrusive. Sometimes they want to be left alone, just like people do. And I check if it's okay with my helpers upstairs – God, or my spirit helpers, whatever you call them. It's nearly always a yes, because this is the work I'm meant to be doing. It may sound strange but I'm really a very down-to-earth person. I just happen to have a gift.

2

I hold my pendulum in front of the animal to get answers to my questions. If it swings clockwise it's yes; anti-clockwise is no. It's quick, it gives factual answers. Then I take time to tune into the animal and see if it has anything to say for itself. That can take time. I either hear words in my head or get the feeling that the animal is experiencing. Sometimes it's quite a laugh, particularly if the animal is communicating something funny about its owner, and sometimes it will reduce me to tears.

3

I've had conclusive proof. A woman left her dog alone during the day and wanted to know if there was anything she could do to make him more comfortable. He said, 'No, I'm fine – I spend the day on the sofa.' She said, 'I know he spends most of the time on the sofa. Although he's in his chair when I walk through the door, there's always a hot place in the sofa cushions.' The dog said one other thing. He said, 'It really irritates me the way she keeps talking when she does the washing-up.' His owner laughed. 'I do talk a lot,' she said. 'Maybe he doesn't like it that I've got my back to him.'

4

For the last two years I've worked with Laszlo, the chief vet at Budapest Zoo. He asked me to look at a sick emu which he called Bonzai. I investigated. I used my pendulum and, when I came to its heart, got a very definite response. I tried to remember my anatomy lessons and came up with the right ventricle in the heart. Laszlo looked at me with a smile: 'I don't think you've got that quite right,' he said. Six months later he rang me. Little Bonzai had died. He had examined the body and found that the cause of the trouble was a blocked right ventricle. 'Now we listen,' Laszlo said.

5

Occasionally I am contacted by vets in England. Like once about Montsy the dog. He was four days from being destroyed. From his behaviour they thought he was either mad or bad. He just didn't know how to behave. 'What does behave mean?' he asked. And he didn't like his name. So I sent off some pills for him and his owners. And we gave him a different name. Now he's a lovely boy. An animal's problems can be related to what's going on with their owners. So the owners get remedies too.

6

I tend to have just one main meal a day, in the evening with wine or whisky. I don't have fried foods. I don't enjoy them anyway. I love vegetables but I do eat meat. I went off beef a long time ago because I could smell the fear in the animal. I do feel guilty about not being a vegetarian, but then I think that God put animals on the earth for us to domesticate and eat, so why waste them? I can't bear waste. I recycle everything I can – from silver paper to clothes.

7

If I kept my mind open to everything all the time, I would be dead in a day – I couldn't go in an underground train because I'd pick up all the negativity and tension. So I close myself down. Even so, by the evening I am tired. I have to look after a sick cat so I tend not to go out. I watch the programmes I've recorded during the day. I love that fast-forward button – you can watch four hours in two. I fall asleep in the chair and wake up much later with the cat on my lap.

Part 2

You are going to read an extract from the biography of a very successful woman. For questions **8–14**, choose the answer (**A**, **B**, **C** or **D**) which you think fits best according to the text.

Margaret's school-days

In her way, she lived and breathed politics from the very start. Her father, Alfred Roberts, was a shopkeeper and a local politician. 'Mr Roberts,' said the report her school sent to Oxford University in 1943, 'who is a local tradesman and a governor of this school, has a family of two girls for whom he has done his utmost
5 in preparing them for careers. I have every confidence in recommending her as I feel quite sure her family will make every effort to ensure her future success.'

So this is not a rags-to-riches story but one which seems to have begun as it meant to go on. Dreda Chomacki, who still lives where she was born, was brought up fifty yards away from the Roberts' corner shop, and has known her
10 since primary school days. Was Margaret Roberts a serious person even then?

Chomacki: 'Quite a serious girl, yes. Not so serious that she didn't play with other children, because I remember games like hide and seek, but I think she was more serious than most children of that age. At the secondary school, I always remember her bulging satchel; it would never close, and mine never
15 seemed to have anything in it. But I wouldn't think she had a deprived childhood. I remember parties that I went to at the shop.'

Margaret Wickstead, another contemporary, also recalls a serious girl.

Wickstead: 'I think I can first remember her at a lecture we had, when she must have been in her fourth year. The well-known author and lecturer Bernard
20 Newman came to talk about spies, and gave a very amusing lecture. At the end he asked for questions in the usual way and instead of a sixth-former standing up, this young, bright-eyed, fair-haired girl from the fourth year stood up and asked him a question. But the thing that rather annoyed her contemporaries was that she asked him these questions in almost parliamentary language: "Does the
25 speaker think so and so?"'

Looking back with the benefit of hindsight, Dreda Chomacki found little early evidence of Margaret Roberts' potential.

Chomacki: 'Strangely enough, looking in old school magazines, rarely can I find any reference to Margaret. She obviously must have been quite prominent,
30 but it's hard to find any records of her work, really. I've often looked back and thought, surely I would find Margaret's name, but not very often.'

8 What part did Alfred Roberts play in his daughter's early life?

    A He worked as hard as he could to help her.

    B He was too busy in his shop and in local politics to be able to do much.

    C He recommended her for university.

    D He brought her up to work as a shopkeeper.

9 What do we find out about Dreda Chomacki?

    A She was brought up away from Margaret but knew her at school.

    B She grew up in the same place as Margaret.

    C She lives in the exact place where Margaret was born.

    D She moved to a house only fifty yards away from Margaret's.

10 Dreda Chomacki thought that Margaret was a serious girl at school because

    A she didn't play with other children.

    B she was determined to become rich.

    C she always took so many things to school with her.

    D she had an exceptional memory for facts.

11 Why was Bernard Newman invited to Margaret's school?

    A He had been a spy and had written a book about them.

    B He helped the pupils with their reading in a very amusing way.

    C He tested the pupils on their reading and writing.

    D He had written books and was a celebrity guest speaker.

12 What annoyed the other girls at school after the lecture?

    A Margaret spoke herself instead of letting an older girl speak.

    B Margaret did not speak how the other girls would have spoken.

    C Margaret didn't seem to appreciate how amusing the lecture was.

    D Margaret was discourteous towards the lecturer.

13 In looking back over her school days, Dreda finds that

    A not much was written down about Margaret.

    B Margaret was not referred to much at school.

    C the evidence of what Margaret did at school has been hidden.

    D Margaret's name has been taken off old school records.

14 Which statement best describes the young Margaret Roberts?

    A She was a very different girl from all the others.

    B She was slightly different in character from the other girls.

    C She was a poor girl who had little potential.

    D She was a serious girl who could be very amusing.

Part 3

You are going to read a magazine article based on an interview with the film star Demi Moore. Eight sentences have been removed from the article. Choose from the sentences **A–I** the one which fits each gap (**15–21**). There is one extra sentence which you do not need to use. There is an example at the beginning (**0**).

Moore than beautiful

Goodness Demi Moore is small! | **0** | **I** | How on earth did she get to be a star? I mean, she has some obvious disadvantages: her skin is really not very good; her eyes (those famous green eyes) are more piercing than beautiful; her build is very unusual. She really is like a child: like an anorexic 12-year-old. There is *something* about her, though.

| **15** | She has a trick of closing them very slowly (she is said to be blind in the left one) and, when she does this, time slows down and those clear eyes opening and shutting dominate your vision.

What else? Well, there is this amazing difference between the way she is and the way she looks on the screen. You probably have an image of her as a bionic woman: earnest, humourless, straining with muscle. | **16** | Yet when I saw her, she didn't appear to have any muscles at all.

But the big mystery is, of course, why she is a star at all. I'm not saying she is ugly: she is obviously better looking than most people. | **17** | That was the problem for me. As she is small and not-quite-beautiful, why is she continually chosen by producers to play beautiful women for enormous salaries?

Perhaps it is sheer determination. She turns out – rather refreshingly – to have many insecurities about almost everything,

including her looks, education, personality and body. | **18** | 'I don't know that I'm determined not to fail,' she told me, 'as much as I'm determined, with anything I put myself into, to know that at the end of the day I've given everything I can.'

She certainly seems to like parts that reflect this determination. Her part as Lt. Jordan O'Neil in *GI Jane* is undoubtedly remarkable in that respect. | **19** | During the filming, Moore refused to use a double for the hard, dirty bits, where the actors were forced to freeze in the sea for hours and run for miles in the blazing sun. | **20** |

Her account of her training confirmed my view of how much she likes to achieve her self-imposed goals – such as stardom, for instance. But she says she was never sure she would make it as a star. | **21** | Does she think so now? 'In general, over time, things that were important are less so. When you're a child, nothing's good, nothing's right, it's got to be better and got to be different – and then you grow and, if you're fortunate, you find other, more important priorities.' Does the dissatisfaction go away completely? 'It pops up every once in a while and I say: "Oh, what a waste of time. Such a waste of time!"'

A In *GI Jane* she looked like a bodybuilder.

B In the film, O'Neil is determined to be the first woman to finish the three-month training to join the special operations team despite everyone else being determined she should fail.

C The significance of this story seemed to have escaped her.

D 'I never felt I had anything that was good enough.'

E But not actually better looking in the flesh than on screen, I think.

F When she talks to you, she fixes you with those green eyes and you start to see … *something*.

G She also claimed she didn't get any privileges, apart from being driven to locations in a car instead of a bus.

H On the other hand, she is totally determined not to fail, though she doesn't put it that way.

I When you meet her it's like looking down the wrong end of a telescope.

Part 4

You are going to read an extract from a brochure about courses at the Business School of a UK university. For questions **22–35**, choose from the courses (**A–E**). Some of the courses may be chosen more than once. When more than one answer is required, these may be given in any order. There is an example at the beginning (**0**).

Which course(s) would be most suitable for someone who

would like to master some common business computer programs?

| 0 | D |

is interested in travel to a different continent?

| 22 | |

wants to learn how to use computers in business?

| 23 | | | 24 | |

wants to study a language without going abroad?

| 25 | |

might need a lot of individual attention, help and support?

| 26 | |

likes a teamwork problem-solving approach to tasks?

| 27 | |

wants to study marketing and information technology?

| 28 | |

would like to undergo practical business training in a British company?

| 29 | |

would like to create computer software packages?

| 30 | |

would like to combine cultural studies with business studies?

| 31 | |

would like to study German at advanced level?

| 32 | |

has already been in business for some time?

| 33 | |

does not want to do a degree course?

| 34 | | | 35 | |

The Business School

The Business School is currently in the forefront of many developments in the field of business and management. It is developing a range of new courses to provide greater opportunities for specialist study, matched to the needs of employers and students.

A   Business Administration – BA Hons

This course is particularly suitable for people with substantial work experience, or for those who prefer not to take a year's work placement as part of the degree. The course lasts three years.

Year 1 introduces you to essential business disciplines. In Year 2 you will be introduced to the professional pathway which you intend to follow. You may choose from marketing, personnel management and industrial relations, business economics, accounting and finance. These pathways are supported by economics and law and a range of options (e.g. consumer law, intermediate French).

In the final year, you will continue to study from a number of options related to your chosen specialist pathway. These are designed to cover a range of professional interests and enable you to follow a course which you can shape to meet your personal requirements and your wider interests.

B   Business Studies – BA Hons

This course is unit-based and enables you to make your final honours choice in Semester 4. The first year incorporates the range of business functions, including accounting, marketing, operations, law and economics. These are combined with the application to business of computing, information technology and the behavioural sciences.

Student choice is then extended by the introduction of options and elective subjects. All students studying a language, and some who are not, go abroad for their industrial year, usually to France, Mexico or Spain. Others may go to the USA, Ireland or Australia. Individual initiative in obtaining such placements is encouraged, but most traineeships are in the UK and obtained through the university, which has long-standing associations with many firms and organisations. You must complete one full year of industrial placement to qualify for the BA Business Studies.

C   International Business (Europe) – BA Hons

This degree is a full-time, three-year programme which includes study abroad. An integral part of the degree is a placement for one semester, during your second year, with a university in one of the countries appropriate to the languages which you will be studying.

You will also study the history and culture of Eastern and Central Europe, an understanding of which is vital for successful business transactions in that region. You will also study German, which will be available for complete beginners and at a more advanced level.

In your final year you will follow a core course in business strategy and complete a project which will reflect the skills and knowledge which you have acquired on the course.

D   Accounting – Foundation Course

An examination pass for this course allows you to be considered for transfer to the second year of the BA Business Studies programme. The course is modular and covers a range of subjects. Each subject is taught for a minimum of one hour a week in lectures, and one hour a week in tutorials or seminars. Coursework is an essential element of the assessment in all modules. A module in information technology emphasises 'hands-on' experience of popular business software packages.

If you have difficulties initially, we provide remedial tutorials and you also have a personal tutor to help you throughout your course.

E   Business Information Technology

This course is for those who want to apply information systems and technology to the needs of business. It has three main areas of study: business structure and management, information technology, and information systems development.

You will learn how a business works and how to apply information technology in a business context. You will also learn the tools and techniques required for developing information systems and will use rapid application development tools to develop software applications and to bring new ideas quickly to life. You will learn how to work with others and understand the importance of interpersonal skills in the effective implementation of business systems.

This is a practical course where skills and knowledge are applied to real-life scenarios through case studies, group work and individual assignments.

Practice test 3

You are going to read an article about how to prepare for success. Choose the most suitable summary sentence from the list **A–I** for each part (**1–7**) of the article. There is one extra summary sentence which you do not need to use. There is an example at the beginning (**0**).

A	Worrying what others think is no recipe for success.
B	Sympathy is no substitute for success.
C	Reliability and attention to detail are important factors.
D	Being unprepared is a poor excuse.
E	Preparing for the worst will result in the best.
F	No sacrifice is too great for the world's best.
G	For one champion, preparation has been a way of life.
H	Hard work is the key.
I	Luck doesn't last – it's preparation that counts.

The 110% solution

0 I

There are those who achieve success as the result of a chance: being in the right place at the right time. But this kind of success is usually short-lived. If you want to stay on top you have to work at it, which usually means giving a lot of time and energy to preparation. I've never met a truly successful person who wasn't 110% prepared. Once you realise the advantage that exceptional preparation gives, it becomes a lifelong habit.

1

Ivan Lendl was a case in point. He thought about every side to his game, whether it was a playing strategy against an opponent, or his diet, or fitness regime or when he scheduled his sleep. That attitude touched every part of his life. The first time I met Ivan, I was impressed that he knew exactly where he was going to be in six months' time, even though this is not uncommon for a top performer. But what really astonished me was when he told me he also knew the airline and flight number he was taking to the city in question. That is how he goes about everything.

2

Jackie Stewart, too, is always very well prepared. If he says he will meet you eleven weeks from Monday at 10.30 at your Chicago office, you have no need to reconfirm the appointment. Jackie will be there. Much of this, I am sure, he picked up during his racing career, where checking the safety and performance details before he took the wheel was a matter of life or death. Jackie has never abandoned that discipline in his other pursuits. It is one ingredient that made him a champion.

3

One reason many of us aren't prepared is that we rarely get credit for it. Preparation is something we do outside the spotlight. And if anyone *does* find out we have prepared intensively to make certain we achieve our goal, we may well be teased. Successful people are also those who have learned to accept teasing as part of being what they are. After all, if you get to the top of your particular profession, you will have the last laugh.

4

Many people are afraid to be prepared: if they are, they lose an excellent excuse when they fail. In sport, you meet athletes who let it be known they are not in top condition for a tournament or game. It relieves the pressure. If they lose, they were not at their best. If they win, they exceed everyone's expectations. This is a classic 50% solution: you win some, you lose some.

5

Then there are the people who do their preparation in public. They constantly tell you how hard they are working. That way, if they fail, it is not because they did not try. This is the 75% solution: prepare well, give it your best, let things turn out as they will. You can be pretty sure that people will feel sorry for you if things go wrong; you may even get more attention and support than the person you were trying to beat. But being consoled as a worthy loser is not the same as glowing with success.

6

The very best performers spend hidden hours to make sure that they are No 1. They don't need or want the world to see them sweat. Ballet dancers train eight hours a day for years so their spins and leaps on stage look effortless. The actor Laurence Olivier would spend weeks memorising his lines until he could recite them without thinking. Only then would he start to rehearse a play.

7

When Christine Brinkley was top model in the world, being photographed for the cover of *Sports Illustrated* swimsuit issue, she would schedule her wake-up call at 2 a.m. knowing that unless she put icepacks on her eyes, which always swelled with sleep, she would not look good enough when the sun broke over the horizon. That was when the light was soft, when the tones showed her off best and the photographer was ready to shoot. This is the 110% solution.

Part 2

You are going to read an article about the early cinema industry. For questions **8–14**, choose the answer (**A**, **B**, **C** or **D**) which you think fits best according to the text.

The American beginnings of the cinema industry

Film is a medium that might have been especially made for America, a vast country which, by the beginning of the twentieth century, had a large immigrant population, many of whom could hardly speak English. These people would have had little use for the theatre, even if they lived within easy distance of one, or for most of the books they
5 could buy because they did not have enough English. But the movies – the silent movies – these they could all understand, so what America had more than any European country was a huge captive audience, a large proportion of them pretty well uneducated. And what these people wanted were simple stories in which, irrespective of the fact they couldn't understand the captions, the action told all.
10 In feeding the growing demand for screen entertainment, America was greatly helped by the First World War. Between 1914 and 1918 the making of films was not exactly high on the list of any European country's priorities. Films continued to be made but not to the same extent as before, and to fill the gap in foreign imports, America had to increase its own production. By the end of the decade, with
15 Hollywood now firmly established as the centre of the industry, America was well on its way to monopolising the world market.
But if by the beginning of the 1920s America was the world leader in film production, it was not then – nor has it been since – in the lead when it comes to developing film as an art form. Hollywood is not interested in art; it is interested in money and the
20 two rarely go together. To Hollywood film is, and really always has been, an industry. There is nothing about this attitude that should make us look down on it. The maker of decent, serviceable and mass-produced furniture is not to be looked down on because he isn't Chippendale.* You might wish he were, but that is another matter. So Hollywood quickly recognised film as an entertainment medium with a unique ability
25 to put people onto seats and money in the pockets of producers, distributors and cinema managers and, mostly, left it to others to develop its potential as an art form.
Generally speaking, the efforts to extend the boundaries of film – to show that it could do more than car chases, romance and clowning – were being made elsewhere. In the 1920s in Germany, for example, expressionism was an artistic movement which
30 used film as a medium. Expressionism is described in the *Oxford Companion to Film* as 'a movement whose main aim was to show in images man's inner world and in particular the emotions of fear, hatred, love and anxiety'. These days, most serious – and sometimes not so serious – films attempt to do something like that as a matter of course.
35 Meanwhile Russian film-makers were developing advanced techniques in editing and montage – using scenes to give background information, ideas and intellectual points. Hollywood was not slow to learn from its foreign competitors or to take on and adapt their ideas, but with regard to the style and content of film-making, it was and still is far more in the business of learning than of teaching.

* Chippendale was a famous eighteenth-century furniture maker, widely considered to be an artist.

8 Why did the large immigrant population in America prefer cinema to other entertainment media?

    A They did not have theatres close enough to their homes.
    B They could not afford to buy books.
    C The language of other entertainment media was too difficult.
    D The film captions were in simple English.

9 How did the First World War help the American film industry?

    A More films were made in America because fewer European films were made.
    B European films were shorter and poorer in quality.
    C There was a greater demand for films during the war.
    D Film production was given a high priority during the war.

10 What do we learn about the American film industry around 1920?

    A American art films were not as successful as those from other countries.
    B More films were made in America than anywhere else.
    C More films from America were seen in the world than from any other country.
    D The Americans were the first to develop film as an art form.

11 What does the author think about Hollywood?

    A He despises Hollywood's interest in making money.
    B He wishes Hollywood would make decent films.
    C He thinks Hollywood films are no better than furniture.
    D He doesn't see anything wrong in Hollywood's approach.

12 What does *its* in line 26 refer to?

    A an entertainment medium
    B Hollywood
    C film
    D money

13 What do we learn about expressionism in film?

    A It has become a less serious element in films nowadays.
    B Its aims are no longer limited to German films.
    C In the 1920s, most serious films were expressionist.
    D It was about trying to show strange emotions.

14 How has Hollywood responded to its foreign competitors?

    A It has maintained a more businesslike position.
    B It has learned a lot from them about what to put in films.
    C It has responded quickly by copying foreign films.
    D It has tried to teach as much as it has learned.

Part 3

You are going to read the introduction to a book about convent education. Seven paragraphs have been removed from the text. Choose from the paragraphs **A–H** the one which fits each gap (**15–20**). There is one extra paragraph which you do not need to use. There is an example at the beginning (**0**).

There's something about a convent girl

Rosemary Forgan explains what makes a convent education special.

The things you hear, or indeed remember from personal experience, about convent education may strike you as bizarre, inspiring or brutal, according to one's stand on these matters, but what is quite breathtaking to most people is the similarity of the experience.

0 **H**

For decades it must have seemed as if nuns were busying about in every corner of the world, worrying over the length of girls' skirts, urging them to eat unpalatable food and, most important of all, alerting them to the dangers lying in wait in the outside world.

15

The other thing that strikes a lot of people is how, with all the emphasis on humility, modesty and the putting of almost everybody before oneself, the nuns managed to produce so many extraordinarily strong-minded women.

16

There seems little doubt that one aspect of convent education that appeals to parents is the idea of a school uniform. In turn the efforts made by daughters to liven it up a bit, or even to make it a bit more modern, deserve awards for creativity.

17

Nuns seemed to spend a lot of their time like this, doing detective work, looking for some-

thing wrong – based on no more than a feeling that something was going on. On many occasions, of course, their intuition was absolutely right.

18

But what really separated the convent school from any other was the sense of guilt which children were made to feel if they failed to reach the required standards in all things. And of course, unless you are guilty of the sin of pride, you will assume you don't reach the required standard.

19

So much has changed as far as convent schools are concerned that it would probably be difficult for today's convent girls to identify with previous generations of convent girls and their school experiences. Nowadays their manner, their attitudes, their aspirations and ambitions are almost unrecognisable to those educated in previous generations of convent schools.

20

What they haven't had, however, is an education occasionally so insane that one had no choice but to rebel, thus sampling at an early age the heady delights of rebellion! However, maybe today's convent education is closer to the ideals of the early founders, enabling children to fulfil their potential free of the heavy burden of guilt.

A   In a convent school, there was always an enormous temptation to get involved in at least some minor misbehaviour because it took so little to reduce the nuns to a state of complete apoplexy. Only the truly compassionate could have resisted it – and who feels compassion towards their teachers in their teens?

B   A great deal of thought went into those adaptations. Someone at my school worked out that if you wore a very wide elasticated belt over your dress and then buttoned up your cardigan, the overall effect was of a tiny waist and shorter flared skirt (very fashionable at the time). Of course, it was only a matter of time before one of the nuns decided to investigate.

C   The new breed of convent girls appear at best to share a very positive attitude to life and their education. For the most part, academic standards at convents have always been high; but these girls appear to have been encouraged in other ways: to question just about every subject under the sun, and they have been treated as adults. The resulting maturity makes them a credit to their educators.

D   In reality we know the nuns were too busy to spend much time sharing information, even within the same school, much less outside of it, so it is all the more extraordinary that women educated in Melbourne, Bombay, New York and Dublin are as much united by similar memories of their school days as they are separated by years or the continents that divide them.

E   Battles fought over the wearing of school uniform seem to remain high in most people's memory. Britain's highest ranking woman police officer, Assistant Chief Constable Alison Halford, clearly recalls that at her school, eating in uniform, in the street, 'was almost a capital offence'.

F   Yet without that particular side to their character, it is doubtful that many of the original founders of religious orders would actually have got their projects started in the first place, given their battle with men who often had a very negative view of the whole idea.

G   These days guilt is automatically assumed to be a bad thing, so most people get rid of it. This is often a problem for convent-educated women: is the guilt just something left over from their school days, something negative to be got rid of, or is it the sign of a healthy conscience?

H   Unlikely as it sounds, it was as if women in religious orders, not just in Britain but all over the world, conspired to produce an identical female educational system that hardly changed in 150 years.

Part 4

You are going to read an extract from a tour itinerary in New Zealand. For questions **21–35**, choose from the days of the itinerary (**A–G**). Some of the days may be chosen more than once. When more than one answer is required, these may be given in any order. There is an example at the beginning (**0**).

On which day(s) of the tour can you

see art treasures?		**0**	**F**
look at an environmentally friendly power station?		**21**	
go up to the top of a mountain?		**22**	
study New Zealand's industrial past?		**23**	
go underground?		**24**	
travel in an aeroplane?		**25**	
spend the afternoon in a lakeside town?		**26**	
have a chance to buy souvenirs?	**27**	**28**	
see some wildlife?		**29**	
see a fruit-growing region?		**30**	
visit an old place of worship?		**31**	
eat local food?	**32**	**33**	
enjoy a boat trip?	**34**	**35**	

7-day Scenic Explorer tour of New Zealand

A	Day 1 Auckland–Waitomo–Rotorua

Depart Central Hotel at 8.30 a.m. Enjoy panoramic views of Auckland's spectacular harbours and city from the top of Mount Eden, an extinct volcano, before heading south through the rich dairy land of the Waikato province, home of the Maori Queen. At Waitomo caves, enjoy a guided tour of the glow-worm grotto. Back up above ground, travel on to Rotorua, for a two-night stay. Dinner is a special Maori feast, typical of the region, and a Maori concert provides after dinner entertainment.

B	Day 2 Rotorua

Sightseeing today will include a visit to the Agrodome, an amazing agricultural show. See rainbow trout in their natural habitat at Rainbow Springs and visit a specially designed nocturnal house to view the rare flightless kiwi bird. At Whakarewarewa Thermal Reserve see boiling mudpools and geysers. We then visit a model Maori village and meeting house.

C	Day 3 Rotorua–Wellington–Nelson

In the centre is the North Island's volcanic plateau. Visit Wairakei Steam Valley, a unique project using natural heat to generate electricity. See spectacular Huka Falls and picturesque Lake Taupo, New Zealand's largest freshwater lake. Continue south to New Zealand's capital city, Wellington, situated around a magnificent natural harbour. Here board your inter-island cruise to the South Island via Picton. Continue on to the orchard and vineyard region of Marlborough, where you will enjoy afternoon tea and wine tasting at one of New Zealand's top wineries.

D	Day 4 Nelson–Franz Josef Glacier–Queenstown

Today drive to the rugged West Coast and on to Punakaiki to view the fascinating pancake rock formations and blowhole. Visit Shantytown, a replica of an old mining town and ride on a bush train. Journey south along the coastline and through the dense rain forests past Lake Ianthe and Mapourika before entering Westland National Park and sighting Franz Josef Glacier. Travel along the shores of Lake Hawea for lunch at the beautiful holiday resort of Queenstown. For the rest of the day, enjoy at your leisure the natural beauty and attractions. Have a go at watersports on the lake or relax and go shopping. For dinner this evening there is an endless choice of international and traditional New Zealand restaurants or cafés, or you may like to dine and dance at the Skyline Restaurant.

E	Day 5 Queenstown–Dunedin

A highlight of your holiday will be a launch cruise through Fiordland National Park, viewing Mitre Peak and the magnificent Bowen Falls. Journey on through the coastal township of Riverton, right at the southern end of New Zealand, to Dunedin, known as the 'Edinburgh of the South'. Free time on arrival to visit some of the city's splendid museums. Enjoy a Scottish evening complete with bagpipes and kilts.

F	Day 6 Dunedin–Mount Cook

Visit Olveston House with its fine collection of antiques and early New Zealand paintings. Travelling north, we stop to see the amazing Moeraki Boulders then continue inland to Mount Cook National Park. The breathtaking beauty of Mount Cook rising majestically to 3,754 metres above sea level, known to the Maoris as 'Aorangi', the Cloud Piercer, can be seen from the head of Lake Pukaki. You may wish to take a scenic flight (extra cost) over this awe-inspiring alpine region and land on the mighty Tasman glacier.

G	Day 7 Mount Cook–Christchurch

Our first stop this morning is at beautiful Lake Tekapo to view the Church of the Good Shepherd. Travel via Burke Pass to the leafy city of Christchurch where your tour concludes at approximately 2 p.m. allowing plenty of time to relax on the banks of the River Avon or to do some last-minute shopping before your flight home.

Practice test 4

Part 1

You are going to read an article about the importance of popcorn to the British cinema industry. Choose the most suitable heading from the list **A–I** for each part (**1–7**) of the article. There is one extra heading which you do not need to use. There is an example at the beginning (**0**).

A	Learning to cash in
B	A life saver
C	Pleasure value
D	The cost to the consumer
E	From US beginnings
F	The manager's challenge
G	A poor performer
H	Forget the film!
I	A top seller

Popcorn and the British cinema industry

0 | I |

In the golden fields of Kansas, Britain's biggest cinema success is under production. There are no stars, no special effects, no publicity. And it is still a certain winner, guaranteed to make more money than all but the biggest hit movies. The coming attraction is popcorn. Last year, cinema popcorn sales in the UK and Ireland made £20 million plus, way ahead of most films. Only a handful of extremely successful movies could beat it.

1 | |

If it was not for popcorn, soft drinks and ice cream, British cinema would be as extinct as the music hall. The Cinema Exhibitors Association survey found every single screen in the country needed another source of income just to keep operating. Perhaps three or four films a year make money at the box office. The other films just help cinemas tick over, and pull in people to buy popcorn and sweets.

2 | |

Even when a cinema is showing a must-see film, the operator is working on paper-thin profits. He must fill every seat to cover the film company's costs. Distributors regularly demand half the money taken at the box office; with big films they can charge between 69 percent and 89 percent of the takings. Cinemas still have to pay staff and running costs out of what's left. This is where popcorn and sweets enter the equation.

3 | |

A 500g bag of popping corn from your local supermarket costs 48p and provides about 15 huge cartons – at just over 3p each. Cinema-goers, however, can pay almost £4 for one giant helping. Britain's most expensive cinema is the Odeon, Leicester Square, in London's West End, where prices range from £1.95 for a small carton to £2.95 (medium) and £3.95 (jumbo).

4 | |

TeeGee Snacks supplies seven out of ten British cinemas with its Playtime popcorn. Sales and managing director, Andy Camfield, says 'Popcorn is a treat, a real pleasure. There is a mark-up: it's just like the difference between buying wine in a restaurant or at an ordinary shop. It costs 100 percent more.'

5 | |

Managers, keenly aware of the big profit margin, are now using the tricks of the supermarket and fast-food industry to sell more. Some cinemas have a 'fast track' for film-goers who want to buy just popcorn and soft drink. It operates on the same principle as the one basket express check-out at the supermarket.

6 | |

Popcorn at the movies was an idea lifted from the American cinema and refined for home consumption. Now the Americans are copying our style, using less fatty oils. 'It is now very healthy: there's lots of fibre in it,' says Camfield. 'It's not just a pleasure, it's good for you.'

7 | |

'It's even better for the cinema manager,' adds film industry analyst, Ralf Ludemann. He says that cinemas are now huge sweet shops which just happen to show a film and guesses that the mark-up is nearer 400 percent than 100 percent. 'If I were to open a cinema,' he says, 'I would make sure I had a large popcorn and soft drink stand. That way I would be guaranteed a profit, no matter which film is showing.'

Part 2

You are going to read an extract from the biography of Marie Curie, known as 'Manya' when she was a child. For questions **8–14**, choose the answer (**A**, **B**, **C** or **D**) which you think fits best according to the text.

Marie Curie's school-days

Manya's school was an odd place and she learned odd things: how, for instance, to do what you are forbidden to do; how to hide your disobedience quickly; how to seem to be doing what you are not; how to fool government inspectors.

One day her class of twenty-five were having a delicious history lesson –
5 a much more delicious history lesson than other children have ever had because it was a forbidden lesson. All the twenty-five and their teacher knew it was forbidden.

There they sat, the twelve-year-olds. Their ears were all stretched, left ear listening hard for every word of history, right ear quick to catch the first tinkle of
10 a certain door bell. Teacher and pupils were waiting, working, waiting to be caught!

Manya was in the middle of answering a question. On this occasion she was telling what she had learned of the Polish king, Stanislas Auguste.

'He was a clever and highly educated king, a friend of poets and artists. He
15 understood the causes of Poland's weakness and tried to make her strong, but alas, he had no courage ...' Even Manya knew that a king should have courage and her voice was full of fierce regret, the fierce regret of a twelve-year-old who understood quite a lot. Tang—, tang—, ting, ting. Everybody shivered once. Everybody moved quickly. Their teacher piled up her Polish books, every child
20 piled up her exercise books and her Polish history books. The five whose duty it was gathered all the books into their aprons and carried them quickly to the boarders' bedrooms. The rest got their needlework and were making exquisite buttonholes in cotton squares as if they had never done anything else.

The Russian inspector came in accompanied by the unhappy headteacher,
25 who had not been able to prevent his walking fast, and was in a panic for fear that the warning bell, with its two long rings and two short, had not given the children time to hide their disobedience. But there was no sign of anything but needlework.

The inspector sat down heavily. In silence, he looked at the children through
30 his glasses and glanced swiftly at the book the teacher had laid open on the desk with a bored air.

'You were reading aloud while they worked?' he asked. 'What's the book?'
'Krylov's *Fairy Tales*. We have just begun it today.'
The inspector knew that Russian book well and sincerely approved of it. He
35 was very well satisfied with what he saw and felt that he was making a real success of his department.

8 What was odd about Manya's school?

    A The pupils were encouraged to deceive the school inspector.
    B The pupils had to disobey the teacher.
    C The school building was strange.
    D The pupils wrote their own rules.

9 What do we learn about the history lesson?

    A It was about disobedience.
    B It was the best history lesson in the school.
    C It was on the subject of food.
    D It was against the rules.

10 Why were the pupils listening for the bell?

    A It meant the end of the lesson.
    B They wanted the teacher to be caught.
    C It meant the inspector was coming.
    D They wanted to finish their needlework to show the inspector.

11 How did Manya feel while answering the question?

    A frustrated because she didn't know enough about the history she was studying
    B upset because King Auguste had not had enough courage
    C sad and angry because she couldn't finish answering the question
    D annoyed that the king had not made her strong

12 What happened when the bell rang?

    A Some children went to their bedroom while others piled up books.
    B Children moved about in a disorganised way.
    C All the children collected up books, moving quickly because of the cold.
    D All the children put the forbidden books away, according to a precise routine.

13 How did the headteacher feel when she entered the classroom with the inspector?

    A She was discontented that the children had done nothing except make buttonholes.
    B She was pleased that the children had had time to hide their needlework.
    C She was relieved that the children had changed the appearance of the classroom quickly enough.
    D She was afraid that the inspector had heard the warning bell.

14 Why was the inspector satisfied?

    A He thought he had had an influence on the teaching.
    B He liked listening to fairy tales.
    C He couldn't see any needlework.
    D He had given the class plenty of warning of his arrival.

Part 3

You are going to read an article about tourism in the Seychelles, a group of islands in the Indian Ocean. Eight sentences have been removed from the article. Choose from the sentences **A–I** the one which fits each gap (**15–21**). There is one extra sentence which you do not need to use. There is an example at the beginning (**0**).

A fragile sanctuary

Nobody visited the Seychelles much until 1971 when Malé airport was opened and the world could flood in. Now more than half the country's foreign exchange earnings come from tourism. **0** | **I** |

Coming fairly late into the tourism business means that the painful lessons of the older world have been well studied. The beauty and unspoilt nature of the islands are carefully protected. **15** Patrols clean the beaches daily and the sea is constantly monitored for signs of pollution which, when detected, are quickly dealt with.

16 Because the amount of visitors must be limited to protect the environment, the quality of the tourist matters a great deal. Lindsay Chong Seng, a highly committed conservationist in the Ministry of Tourism, considers the economics extremely important: you have to earn as much as you can from each tourist if numbers are to be kept down. 'A perfect tourist is active, hires a car, flies to other islands, takes boat trips, eats out, goes diving, spends money. We don't just want to be a beach resort. **17** This has been the fate of all too many tourist resorts in the Mediterranean, with disastrous consequences.'

Quality visitors are also those who come mainly to appreciate and enjoy the Seychelles' natural beauty. This can sometimes mean discomfort. **18** 'If it rains, that's nature, that's good. If the wind blows seaweed up on the beaches, that's nature. They say they come to see nature, they've got to put up with it.'

19 The international travel business has, over the last twenty years, made the mistake of letting the Seychelles be sold in Europe as a 'holiday paradise' and, in so doing, they miss the point.

Tourists are now going who should probably not bother – like ladies in elegant shoes who will not follow muddy walkways through the wetland nature reserves; or the man in the glass-bottomed boat who, looking at the fish city beneath him, could only ask if the specimens could be eaten or not. Many others, more inclined for adventure and safari and the wonders of the world, do not go. **20** Probably some rich, green-minded Westerners avoid it because of a guilty feeling that tourism spoils such places. **21**

A   Not all do so.

B   When you get mass tourists without a lot of spending money, all you find is that the shops do no business and the local bus service is overcrowded.

C   No Seychelles hotel is allowed to rise above the surrounding palm trees and none may get rid of waste into the sea.

D   Atterville Ceydras, the nature warden on one of the islands, says that tourists have got to accept nature.

E   There are plenty of other more exotic, more exciting destinations.

F   It is a very difficult target to achieve.

G   After a brief period of package holidays and mass tourism, the current policy is to attract the 'quality visitor'.

H   But in this case tourism need not, and poverty surely would.

I   This is an industry which could, if not managed properly, destroy the environment.

Part 4

You are going to read a pamphlet about choosing a pet cat. For questions **22–35**, choose from the breeds of cat (**A–E**). Some of the breeds may be chosen more than once. When more than one answer is required, these may be given in any order. There is an example at the beginning (**0**).

Of which breed(s) of cat is the following stated?

They are unique in their habits.		**0** **B**
They are easy to look after.		**22**
They can have two-tone fur.		**23**
They need attention every day.		**24**
They have unusual markings.		**25**
They grow thick winter coats.	**26**	**27**
They need to get out and about a lot.	**28**	**29**
They are quite big.	**30**	**31**
They need a lot of love.		**32**
They can be quite destructive.		**33**
They are clever.		**34**
They can have unusual eye colouring.		**35**

Choosing your pedigree cat

Although the differences between breeds of pedigree cats are less pronounced than in dogs, the breeds nevertheless do show noticeable variations in appearance and temperament.

A	**Persian Longhair**

You may encounter three different combinations of eye colour in the white Persian Longhair. There are the blue-eyed and orange-eyed variants and you may also come across the odd-eyed white, which has one blue eye and one orange eye. Such cats are usually deaf in the ear corresponding to the blue eye. A wide range of colours exists within the Persian Longhair category. These are all large cats, with round, massive faces and placid, affectionate natures. You will need to be prepared to wipe their faces regularly, as they sometimes suffer from tear-staining, because of the flattened shape of their faces, and food deposits may accumulate in the fur around their mouth. Regular, daily cleaning is equally essential.

B	**Turkish Van**

The Turkish Van is a breed with a longish coat and distinctive markings. These cats are unusual in that they are the only breed that appears actively to like swimming. The breed originates from the southeast of Turkey around the shores of Lake Van, which is an area where the temperature varies quite markedly through the year, with the summers often proving very hot, while the winters can be bitingly cold. These extremes of temperature are reflected in the cat's coat. In the spring, the cats shed much of their long fur, which then regrows during the autumn. Their coloration is a distinctive shade of chalky white, with restricted markings present on the head, ears and tail.

C	**Norwegian Forest Cat**

Another breed that undergoes a fairly marked change in appearance depending on the season is the Norwegian Forest Cat, a long-haired breed that has been established for centuries in Scandinavia and is now becoming better known in other parts of the world. In the winter, when their fur is at its longest, a thick collar is evident around the neck. These are intelligent, hardy and active cats, which do well even in wet weather, with their coats having distinct water-repellent qualities.

D	**Oriental Shorthair**

Blending characteristics of the Siamese with solid coloration, Oriental Shorthair cats come in a huge range of varieties to choose from, which has helped to ensure their popularity. Interestingly, the blue-eyed white form, called the Foreign White, is unusual in that these cats are not generally afflicted by the deafness associated with other blue-eyed, pure white cats. In terms of character, Oriental Shorthair cats tend to mature rapidly and positively demand affection, becoming very attached to their owners. These cats also tend to be athletic by nature, and they must have plenty of exercise, otherwise they may set out to amuse themselves, by shredding the curtains in a room, for example.

E	**British and American Shorthair**

These breeds are both considerably larger than the average cross-bred cat. Male cats in particular develop large chins as they mature, which adds to their impression of substance. Care of the cats is quite straightforward and they make very good pets. You will also have a wide range of colours to choose from, including variants such as the Red Tipped, which you are unlikely to encounter in ordinary shorthairs. The fur of these cats is tipped, creating a reddish shade, which contrasts with the white underfur.

Practice test 5

You are going to read an article about a family being educated while on a world cruise. Choose the most suitable heading from the list **A–I** for each part (**1–7**) of the article. There is one extra heading which you do not need to use. There is an example at the beginning (**0**).

A	Dealing with numbers
B	Learning by doing
C	Doing things the hard way
D	Matching places and projects
E	A personal record
F	Our first lesson
G	A question of space
H	Team entertainment
I	A way of life

Home-schooling on a world cruise

0 | I

I've never believed that the only way to get an education is to sit at a desk with four walls around you. The world is our classroom and our home – a 41-foot sailing boat – takes us there. My husband Tom and I dreamed of sailing around the world before our daughters were even born. Their arrivals only increased our desire to live the cruising lifestyle – a way of life that has given us the opportunity for lots of quality and quantity family time. Educating our two daughters while living afloat on our sailing boat has added a wonderful new dimension to our lives.

1

We started out years ago with a kindergarten correspondence course for our daughter Kate. It's what most cruising families use, I was told, but as Kate zoomed through the entire year's course in a matter of two months, we realised that a pre-packaged school was not what she needed. Kate's gifted mind needed to be challenged, excited, sent into orbit. We devised our own curriculum for the rest of the year.

2

Choosing our own course of study was great fun. We looked at where we would be sailing to during the school year (or where we would be stopping to work) and all sorts of topics of interest presented themselves. For example, while cruising down the East Coast to Florida, we chose space exploration for a unit of study. Our studies included both fictional and non-fictional reading, experiments and writing assignments. The finale was watching a shuttle launch from Cape Canaveral and visiting the Kennedy Space Centre museums.

3

Our maths studies are fairly traditional but we find it easy (and fun!) to put our maths skills to everyday use on board. How exciting to find out where in the world you are located by measuring angles of stars and planets above the horizon or determining your position on a chart by calculating such things as speed, time travelled and course!

4

Both girls keep a diary and a nature journal. My daughter Kate has been writing, editing and publishing a monthly newsletter for the past two years. She sends it to friends and relatives who are able to keep up with our sailing and school activities. It may also contain poetry, weather reports, jokes, artwork, etc. She is quite proud of both her writing accomplishments and her computer skills that she uses to produce her newsletter.

5

We do miss out on a few things that most home-schooled children are able to take advantage of and which would perhaps make our academic life easier. Our home afloat is small. School is held on a small dining table and it's difficult, if not impossible, to leave artwork, science experiments or projects 'until later'. We also have limited room for school books and so those we have must be chosen carefully. Perhaps the thing we miss the most when travelling is not always having access to a library. We hope to upgrade our notebook computer to one with CD ROM soon. Imagine having resources like encyclopaedias and atlases all in a small enough format to fit on the boat!

6

But the advantages of our floating school far outweigh any disadvantages. Part of the reason we cruise is for the wonderful opportunities to learn about the world around us. Hands-on learning experiences we get from hiking through a rain forest, snorkelling over a coral reef, visiting historic ruins, shopping in foreign markets or participating in local festivals are an important part of our schooling.

7

We look forward to the chance to get together with other home-schooled cruisers. This past year we sailed for nearly four months with seven children from three boats with another dozen or more from all parts of the world joining in our group for several days or weeks at a time. The children put on a play – doing everything from acting to making costumes and making a stage on a nearby island. The play was a big success, watched by 15 or so parents and friends.

Part 2

You are going to read an extract from a popular novel, *Autumn Always Comes*. It is about a Spanish girl visiting England for the first time. For questions **8–14**, choose the answer (**A**, **B**, **C** or **D**) which you think fits best according to the text.

Arriving in London

The plane turned slowly and she looked down at the collection of dolls houses and duck ponds.

The 'No Smoking' sign flashed on. People fastened their seatbelts, packed away paperbacks and magazines, and above the roar of the engines conversation
5   seemed to hum and ripple.

Juana looked down through the cabin window again at the toy town, wondering what it would be like to really live there for six whole weeks. She'd read about England, of course. Everybody had read about it at school.

She knew, for example, it was a constitutional monarchy; that London was the
10 capital with about six million people living in it; that the currency was the pound sterling, the main agricultural products dairy farming, livestock and fishing – and that her mother wanted her to bring home a lambswool sweater and some jars of marmalade. But none of that made it seem any more touchable, and she trembled suddenly – a sick feeling, that had nothing to do with the plane's dropping height,
15 was grasping hold of her.

She'd been away from home before, of course. Last summer she'd spent a fortnight in Mallorca with Katerine. And the summer before that, when she was only fourteen, she and Dolores Camino had actually been allowed to go on a school trip to Madrid.

20 But that was different. Katerine and Dolores were friends. She'd known them and their families all her life. They talked the same language and understood the same jokes. In the spring holidays she and Dolores had even fallen in love with the same boy.

In England, in London, there would only be Sandie to talk to – whom she'd
25 written to, but never met.

The sick feeling turned to near panic.

She'd boasted such a lot about the English trip and told everybody how she'd think of them doing the same old boring summer things while she was busy shopping in the King's Road and waving to Prince Charles.

30 Now it was all here and happening, and as the Iberia plane touched down and began to roll along the runway she took a deep breath and whispered: 'Good luck!'

8 What did Juana do when the 'No Smoking' sign came on?

   A She put her things away, ready for landing.

   B She looked out of the window and thought about her holiday.

   C She continued her conversation, despite the roar of the engines.

   D She looked at some little toys she had brought with her.

9 How did Juana feel about going to stay in England?

   A She was confident because she knew so much about England.

   B She was worried about the things she had to buy for her mother.

   C She didn't feel prepared for it, even though she knew a lot about the country.

   D She had no strong feelings but felt unwell because of the movement of the plane.

10 What does the extract tell you about Juana's holidays before this one?

   A She had been on holiday twice before without her parents.

   B She had been to England before.

   C She had had several holidays at her friends' houses.

   D She had been to Mallorca when she was fourteen.

11 What was Juana's relationship like with her friends?

   A She had three close friends: Katerine, Dolores and Sandie.

   B She was a close friend of Katerine and Dolores while Sandie was only a pen-friend.

   C She was not as close to Katerine and Dolores as they were to each other.

   D Of all her friends, Sandie was the only one she could talk to.

12 Before leaving, what had Juana told her friends?

   A that she would miss them while she was in England

   B that she would be envious of them while she had to do boring things like shopping

   C that she would remember to buy presents for them and even to say hello to Prince Charles for them

   D that she would remember them while she was enjoying herself and having fun

13 What does *it* in line 30 refer to?

   A the boring summer

   B Juana's arrival at the airport

   C Juana's trip to England

   D shopping and waving

14 Which is the best description of Juana as she arrived in England?

   A She was mystified and curious.

   B She felt apprehensive and unsure.

   C She was sad and regretful.

   D She felt ill and breathless.

Part 3

You are going to read a magazine article about domesticated animals. Seven sentences have been removed from the article. Choose from the sentences **A–H** the one which fits each gap (**15–20**). There is one extra sentence which you do not need to use. There is an example at the beginning (**0**).

Creature comforts

Which is the most successful animal alive today? Is it the lion, yawning and stretching in the midday African sun, king of the jungle with nothing to fear from any other animal? **0** **H** A good case could be made for humans themselves, of course, who have conquered all parts of the world and successfully settled in most of them. **15** This is closely followed by the horse, the pig, the cow, the dog, and all the other domesticated creatures.

These animals have hitch-hiked a ride with humans on the fast track to development. **16** In 1860, humans and domesticated animals represented about five percent of all plant and animal life. Today they are about one fifth, according to biologist Raymond Coppinger of Hampshire College, Massachusetts. 'The domestic animals, the dependent animals, the ones that have made themselves fit in with the existence of humans, they are the success stories in the history of animal development,' he says.

17 Among those who argue that animals should have the same rights as humans, domestication means humans profiting from animals: as they see it,

humans have simply used animals for their own selfish purposes, using increasingly cruel methods. The idea that domestication, instead of serving a human purpose, has actually helped animals to survive and develop is revolutionary and will probably make the animal rights movement even angrier. **18** Coppinger's studies seem to show that it was not humans who decided to take animals from the wild and to domesticate them for their own uses; on the contrary, it was, in the first instance, the animals themselves who approached humans, giving them the idea that animal farming could be to their mutual advantage.

19 Biologists argue that the driving force in all animals is the desire to ensure that you and your future generations survive, and if this is right then it is clear where the benefits to animals lay. **20** Wild cows have been wiped out and wild horses would very likely have been wiped out if it were not for domestication. The move animals made from life in the wild to life with human beings, in settlements, was simply a measure for self-protection and a way of guaranteeing the future of the species.

A This is certain to cause an argument because it denies a central claim of the animal rights movement.

B The continued survival of some kinds of domestic animal is not difficult to understand.

C But the animal that seems to have made the most of its limited opportunities is the domestic sheep.

D Wild sheep today have been almost wiped out.

E Yet there is evidence to support it.

F They have escaped the pressures which would have wiped some of them out and increased their share of the total living matter on earth.

G So if, as it seems, it was animals that took the first step in the process of domestication, agreeing to live with humans on a voluntary basis, what exactly did they get from it?

H Or is it some insect unknown to science, reproducing itself in millions, deep in the Amazon rain forest?

Part 4

You are going to read an information leaflet about working freelance. For questions **21–35**, choose from the freelance jobs (**A–E**). Some of the jobs may be chosen more than once. When more than one answer is required, these may be given in any order. There is an example at the beginning (**0**).

Of which freelance job(s) is the following stated?

A lot of people are trying to work in this area.	**0**	**D**
It involves physical, manual work.	**21**	
It is very important to be punctual with your work.	**22**	
Clients value past experience.	**23**	**24**
It is a good idea to appoint a professional to help build up your business contacts.	**25**	
You need to be careful about how you describe yourself.	**26**	
You may need to know a particular person in order to get work.	**27**	**28**
Research is a key factor in identifying potential clients.	**29**	
You should think particularly carefully about what you do with the money you earn.	**30**	
There are certain tax advantages.	**31**	
Clients may have a negative view of this area.	**32**	
Individual incomes vary enormously.	**33**	
It is important to publicise your services widely.	**34**	
There is a demand for people with a technical speciality.	**35**	

Going freelance

Working successfully as a freelance means more than being competent at what you do, as this round-up shows.

A | Freelancing as a management consultant

The term 'consultant' has been overworked and, in some potential clients' minds, means 'managers who are out of work and looking for a job'. It might be better to describe yourself as 'Expert in ...' or 'Advisor on ...' (whatever the name of the subject or discipline). This will also focus attention right away on your area of expertise – it is very important to be able to describe what you do in as few words as possible. If you can establish your expertise in a subject or area that is in demand, your advice is taken more seriously than that of a management consultant who has never had to put into practice what he advises about.

B | Home and DIY services

Services to the home are mostly concerned with care and maintenance of buildings and repairs to a wide variety of items, ranging from household equipment and gadgets to cars. There are two routes to success that are worth taking. One is to keep your activity clear and simple and not to move outside a definable field of competence. The other is to put that message over in your publicity and to make sure it is seen by possible customers. The opportunities to operate without declaring your income to the authorities are very considerable – though not desirable – which may be one reason why what must be a major freelance field is not well publicised.

C | Photography, illustration and design

In this kind of work nothing impresses clients as much as a successful record. You should begin by looking round for clients who you think would like your work. That is not only a matter of personal contacts, but also of studying media that publish the kind of thing you yourself like and can do. It is in these offices that your work is most likely to make an impact. Taking your work round to potential clients is time-consuming and not everyone is effective in marketing their own work. An agent can be useful here. It means that the commercial side of things is divorced from the personal and artistic rapport which is so important in working with a client on the creative side.

D | Performing arts

Freelancing in this area is extremely competitive. Top names can make a great deal of money – for instance, a star actor can get a very large income from films, stage appearances, commercials and voice-overs. The majority of performers, however, earn much smaller amounts of money. The other factor is that some careers can be relatively short – sportspeople and models, for instance, only have a top earnings life of 10–15 years. Sound investment advice is, therefore, as important as having a good agent, though to judge by the frequency with which performers succeed in losing their hard-earned savings, not many realise this.

E | Journalism and writing

Journalism is a good area for freelancing, particularly if you specialise in a technical subject that attracts a lot of advertising: electronics is, at the moment, a notable case in point. On the other hand, it is very difficult to break into more general fields or into art, music, sport and travel. Newspapers and magazines are not the only possibilities for freelance writers. It is difficult to make money out of books, or even to get published, but writing advertising copy can be very profitable. However, such opportunities are hard to come by and seem to appear through personal contacts. Whatever branch of writing you decide to try, there is one universal principle. Reliability is all, and delivering even fairly boring stuff on time is worth almost any amount of unpunctual genius.

Acknowledgements

The author would particularly like to thank the footballer, Kerry Davis, who provided the article about Rose Reilly, Carmela di Clemente, Charles Crawford, Sara Mather and Mary Curtin, who contributed with help and advice at the early stages of piloting the first edition, and Erica Hall for her expert editing of this second edition.

The author and publishers are grateful to the following individuals and institutions for permission to use copyright material in *Cambridge First Certificate Reading*. While every effort has been made, it has not been possible to identify the sources of all the material used and in such cases the publishers would welcome information from copyright holders.

Text extracts and accompanying illustrations

p. 4 adapted from *An Awfully Big Adventure*, Gerald Duckworth & Company Ltd © Beryl Bainbridge 1991; p. 5 from *Learning from the Perspective of the Comprehender* by Bransford, Stein and Shelton, taken from Anderson and Urquhart, *Reading in a Foreign Language*, reprinted by permission of Addison Wesley Longman Ltd; p. 8 from *Had Enough of Studying?* from *All Clear*, Hobsons Publishing Plc; p. 11 adapted from *The Fun They Had* from *Earth is Room Enough* by Isaac Asimov © 1957 Isaac Asimov, used by permission of Doubleday, a division of Bantam Doubleday Dell Publishing Group, Inc.; pp. 15 & 16 adapted from *Bedford College Prospectus 1995*; p. 19 adapted from *The Opposite Sex* by Anne Campbell, Andromeda Oxford Ltd; p. 27 adapted from *Loved to Death* by Simon Hoggart, BBC *World Magazine*, BBC Worldwide Ltd; p. 32 adapted from *Thomas Cook Holidays Winter Faraway Collection*, December 1994–March 1995, Thomas Cook Holidays; p. 35 adapted from *Animals Before Breakfast* by M. Bowring, W.H. Allen 1978; p. 40 adapted from *Zooooooh!* by Tess Lemmon, *New Internationalist*, January 1991; p. 43 adapted from *Train Your Human*, David & Charles 1979, reprinted by permission of the publishers; pp. 51 & 52 adapted from *Madonna – The Biography* by Matthew Walker, Sidgwick and Jackson; p. 55 adapted from *The Wild Rose of Trani* by Jean Rafferty, *Mail on Sunday, You Magazine*; pp. 62 & 63 adapted from *Computers Kill Off Cinema's Death-defying Stuntmen* by S. McGinty, *The Sunday Times*, 18 May 1997; pp. 67 & 68 adapted from *Secrets of Screen Acting* by P. Tucker, Routledge; p. 80 © Partap Sharma 1985, first published by Andre Deutsch, an imprint of Scholastic Ltd; p. 82 adapted from *How to Get Out* from *The Rat Race Stops Here* by R. Gooch, *Maxim*, June 1995, Dennis Publications; p. 85 *On Location – The Film Fan's Guide to Britain and Ireland* by B. Pendreigh, Mainstream Publishing Co. Ltd; p. 87 adapted from *A Life in the Day of Anne Wilson* by R. Johnson, *The Sunday Times Magazine*, 7 September 1997; p. 88 adapted from *The Thatcher Phenomenon* by Hugo Young and Anne Sloman, BBC Worldwide Ltd; p. 90 adapted from *Twice The Woman She Used to Be* by M. MacDonald, *The Observer, Life Magazine*, 12 October 1997; p. 93 adapted from *University of Greenwich Prospectus*, University of Greenwich, London; p. 95 adapted from *The 110% Solution* by M. McCormack, Chapmans; p. 96 adapted from *100 Best Films of the Century* by Barry Norman, Chapmans; p. 98 adapted from *There's Something about a Convent Girl* by J. Bennett & R. Forgan with permission from Virago Press and Little Ltd; p. 101 adapted from the *Australian Pacific Tours New Zealand Brochure 1995/6*, Australian Pacific Tours (UK Ltd); p. 103 adapted from *Profits Pop as Corn Becomes Star Performer* by N. Luck and J. Burns, *Daily Express*; p. 104 from *The Radium Woman* by Eleanor Doorly, Methuen Children's Books (division of Egmont Children's Books Ltd); p. 106 adapted from *A Fragile Sanctuary* by E. Purves, BBC *World Magazine*, BBC Worldwide Ltd; p. 109 adapted from

Your Kitten's First Year by Don Harper, Quintet Publishing Ltd, London; p. 111 adapted from *A World of Learning* by Barbara Theisen, *Home Education Magazine*; p. 114 adapted from *Creature Comforts* by Nigel Hawkes, BBC *World Magazine*, BBC Worldwide Ltd; p. 117 adapted from *Going Freelance* by G. Golzen, Kogan Page Ltd.

Text permissions researched by Nikki Burton.

Photographs

p. 21: Tony Stone Images/Peter Cade; p. 22: Emma Lee/Life File; pp. 30 & 100: Tony Stone Images/Chad Ehlers; p. 35: John Karmali/Frank Lane Picture Agency; p. 38: Barnaby's Picture Library; p. 40: Terry Whitaker/Frank Lane Picture Agency; p. 48: The Kobal Collection; p. 54: *The Wild Rose of Trani* by Jean Rafferty, *You Magazine*; p. 59: Moviestore Collection; p. 63: Tony Stone Images/Don Morley; p. 83: Colorific!/Michael Yamashita; p. 84: Aquarius/Andrew Cooper; p. 91: The Ronald Grant Archive; p. 92: Telegraph Colour Library; p. 107: Tony Stone Images/Martin Barraud; p. 108: Telegraph Colour Library/Bavaria-Bildagentur.

Photograph re-clearance and picture research by Diane May.

Illustrations

pp. 2, 3, 4, 5, 6 (bottom), 7 (bottom), 9, 10, 12, 13, 14, 16, 17, 18, 20, 22, 23, 25 (top), 28, 31, 37, 39, 41, 42, 44, 45, 47, 50, 53, 56, 58, 61, 64, 66, 69, 71, 72, 75 and 115: Bill Piggins; p. 7 (top): Amanda MacPhail; p. 25 (bottom): Peter Byatt; p. 34: Angela Joliffe; p. 46: Jeremy Long; p. 51: Celia Chester.

Cover illustration by Annabel Wright.